5/10   8 —

Curiosities Series

Colorado
CURIOSITIES

Quirky characters,
roadside oddities &
other offbeat stuff

2nd Edition

D1396853

Pam Grout

Guilford, Connecticut

The prices, rates, and hours listed in this guidebook were confirmed at press time. We recommend, however, that you call establishments to obtain current information before traveling.

To buy books in quantity for corporate use or incentives, call **(800) 962–0973** or e-mail **premiums@GlobePequot.com.**

Photos by Pam Grout unless otherwise noted
Maps by Sue Murray © Morris Book Publishing, LLC
Text design: Bret Kerr
Project manager: John Burbidge

ISBN 978-0-7627-5415-1

The Library of Congress has cataloged the earlier edition as follows:
Grout, Pam.
   Colorado curiosities : quirky characters, roadside oddities & other offbeat stuff / Pam Grout.—1st ed.
     p. cm.—(Curiosities series)
     Includes bibliographical references and index.
     ISBN–13: 978–0–7627–3978–3
     ISBN–10: 0–7627–3978–9
   1. Colorado—Miscellanea. 2. Colorado—Guidebooks. 3. Curiosities and wonders—Colorado. I. Title. II. Series.
     F776.6.G76 2006
     978.8—dc22   2005036461

Printed in the United States of America

10 9 8 7 6 5 4 3 2 1

This book is still for Jim Dick, who dreams of climbing all fifty-four of Colorado's 14-footers

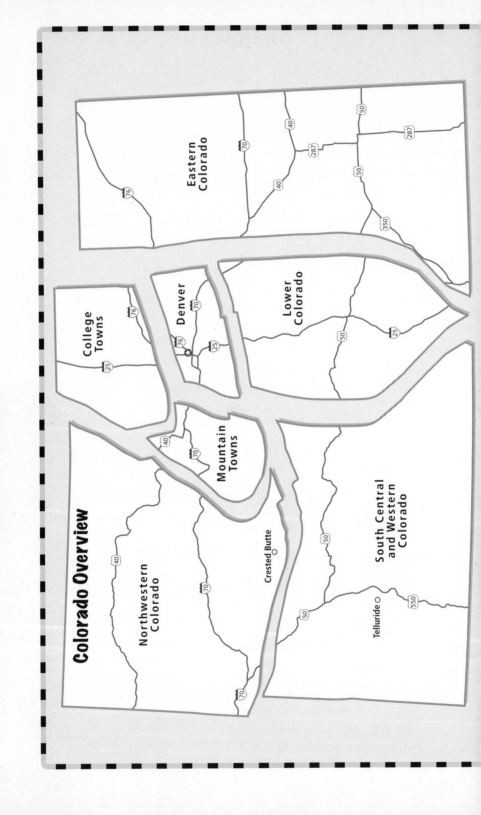

Colorado Overview

Northwestern Colorado

College Towns

Denver

Mountain Towns

Eastern Colorado

Lower Colorado

South Central and Western Colorado

Crested Butte

Telluride

contents

acknowledgments

★ ★

I'd like to give a big group hug to Beth Buehler, Jane Chaney, Rob Strickland, April Prout, Glo Cunningham, and all my other crazy Crested Butte hosts. Thank you for tromping around taking photos, for answering my endless questions, and for demonstrating just how much fun a job can be. I feel compelled to add that I still think my team's entry in the snow-building competition should have placed first.

I'd also like to thank Katie Singer, Ashley Boling (who gives super-fun historical tours of Telluride), Jerry Greene, Iris Willow, Nancy Wicks, Marcie Telander, Patricia Maher, Lori Giggey, Ed Eaton, Doc Phillips, Steph Hilliard, Randi Lowenthal, Roxie from Fruita, Marne Jurgemeyer, Rich Grant, and everyone else from the great state of Colorado who helped me secure photos and other important tidbits.

I'd like to thank Globe Pequot's own Gillian Belnap for her immeasurable patience in dealing with my technological deficiencies, especially my inability to figure out on which side of a photo the blue dot should be adhered. Thanks again to Mary Norris, Erin Turner, John Burbidge, and everyone else at Globe Pequot Press who keeps me from having to get a real job.

And, as always, a big hug to Tasman McKay Grout, my unflappable fifteen-year-old.

preface to the second edition

★ ★

*H*aving the opportunity to revise this book was like pulling a winter coat out of the closet and finding a forgotten $100 bill stuffed in the pocket. By the time an author turns in a manu-script, the last thing he or she wants to do is reread it. Not for a while. After sitting down at a typewriter and opening a vein, as sportswriter Red Smith so famously described the act of writing, an author needs time to breathe, to walk, to think about other things. So to go back to a book four years later and find a $100 bill, well, that's a treat. It could have been a five-spot.

Even more exciting is that the great state of Colorado is every bit as eccentric and quirky today as it was four years ago. In fact, the hardest part about revising this book was deciding which attractions to leave in and which to replace. When you're as attached to Headless Mike and flying fruitcakes as I am, updating a book becomes a regular "Sophie's Choice." I mean, how could anyone entertain the idea of being disloyal to Bishop's Castle or Frozen Dead Guy Days?

All I can say is, "Enjoy!" And look for the sequel.

introduction

I am not eccentric. I'm just more alive than most people. I am an electric eel in a pond of goldfish.

—Edith Sitwell

When you're raised in Kansas like I was, you can't wait to grow up and move to Colorado. It's an indisputable fact, same as pi = 3.1459265, just like "thank you" notes need to be sent after baby showers.

In fact, when you grow up in Kansas, grown-ups don't ask, "What do you want to be when you grow up?" They ask, "Where do you want to be?"

And the answer, for those of us who spent our formative years in the Sunflower State, is pretty much universal: "Colorado." We want to live where we spent our summer vacations—in Estes Park, where we fed peanuts to chipmunks; at the Garden of the Gods, where our dads snapped Polaroids of us pretending to hold up Balanced Rock; at Cripple Creek, where we "booed" the villains at the yearly melodrama.

Of course, back then, we thought we wanted to move west for the mountains, for the air that smelled like something from an aerosol can, for the ski instructors that put Billy Deewater, the wheat farmer's son we all had crushes on, to shame.

But when I finally did move to Colorado, I realized that while the views, the air, and the cute ski instructors are certainly perks, the real beauty of Colorado is in the mindset of the people, in the willingness of Coloradoans to try new things, to step out of the box, to see the world differently than CNN says it is.

While the rest of the country obsesses about unemployment rates, Coloradoans create jobs building horses out of car bumpers, squeezing themselves into 20-inch Plexiglas cubes, and memorizing zip codes. While other states "tsk-tsk" Janet Jackson's breast, Coloradoans skateboard nude, host tele-a-thongs, and throw parties where everyone comes naked except for raincoats. While the politicos fret about high oil prices, Coloradoans build solar ovens, greenhouses, and lawn mowers. I even found a guy in Crawford who built a solar bubble machine.

Checks and balances are what Colorado is all about.

Some blame it on the altitude, say a person's brain goes fuzzy when it resides at 9,800 feet, claim it's not natural to make dragons out of hubcaps, to give awards for beer drinker of the year. All I know is that the people of Colorado know things the rest of the world seems to have forgotten: that having a good time is a good thing, and that viewing life as a grand and glorious adventure is a valuable endeavor.

Eastern Colorado

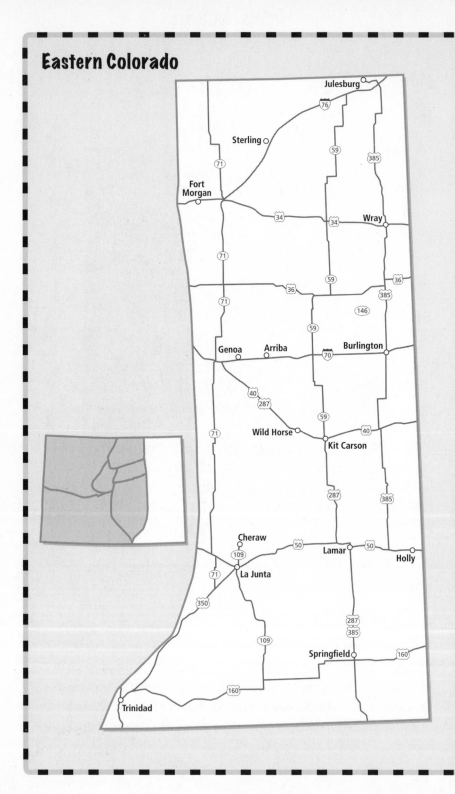

1

Eastern Colorado

Being eastern Colorado *is like being Julia Roberts' sister.*

Julia Roberts has a sister?

See what I mean?

You know that Bette Midler ditty, "Wind Beneath My Wings," the one about being "cold there in my shadow"? Well, that could be the theme song for eastern Colorado. Just look at any Colorado map. Your eye is immediately drawn to all that dramatic green and brown and purple on the western side of the state. It isn't fair. Why should Aspen, Vail, and Telluride get all the glory when Punkin Center, Swink, and Haxton go uncelebrated?

If Comanche Grasslands, Bent's Old Fort, and Junkrassic Park were in any other state, they'd be household names. Tourists would flock. But instead, they pulled the unlucky straw of sitting next door to fifty-four 14,000-foot mountains.

That's the mission of this chapter. To rectify a gross injustice. Eastern Colorado has exotic luxury carousels, the world's longest mural, dinosaur tracks, and prairie chickens who jump in the air, turn circles, and put Jim Carrey's antics to shame.

There also happen to be dozens of jaw-dropping, every-bit-as-stunning hikes in eastern Colorado, only instead of going up, you go down—into canyons with prehistoric petroglyphs and mammoth calabaza plants that dip beneath the prairie. Suffice it to say, Julia Roberts' sister is one heck of a gal.

★ ★

Coulrophobiacs, Enter at Your Own Risk
Arriba

There's a very sound reason why Johnny Depp, Diddy, and Bart Simpson have not yet visited this small town of 224. Namely, because the town's major tourist attraction, one of the world's preeminent clown museums, would make their knees knock, their palms sweat, and their throats swell up with lumps. Diddy includes a "no clown" clause in his concert contracts, Depp suffered clown nightmares as a kid, and as for Simpson, you have to conclude that anyone whose mantra is "Can't sleep, clown will eat me" suffers from a severe case of coulrophobia.

For the 92 percent of Americans who aren't afflicted with clinical clown phobia, there's Grampa Jerry's Clown Museum, a three thousand-plus collection of everything Bozo. Jerry Eder, who started his panic-inducing collection with a pair of porcelain clowns purchased at Circus Circus in Vegas, has clown cookie jars, clown banks, and clown whiskey decanters along with the more unusual glow-in-the-dark clown tattoos, clowns fashioned from neckties, and a hand-painted clown made from a hairball found in a cow's stomach. Eder even has the world's smallest clown, a 1940-something figure that measures in at ⅜-inch. Let's just say Ronald McDonald would feel right at home.

You can't really miss the place. The south-facing side of the small pinkish museum has a big red nose, a smile, and windows with eyeballs. If you call ahead, Grampa Jerry will even provide ice tea or lemonade. Grampa Jerry's Clown Museum is located at 22 Lincoln Avenue; (719) 768-3257.

Life after Death after Death after Death . . .
Burlington

If you go to the Goodland, Kansas, cemetery, you'll find a mausoleum for a man named James Nelson Gernhart. Even though the mausoleum is impressive—one of the biggest memorials in the whole

★ ★

cemetery—nobody in Goodland has ever heard of him.

That's because the retired farmer who bought the plot in the Goodland Cemetery is from Burlington, Colorado, 32 miles away. He liked to say he "wouldn't be caught dead" in his hometown of Burlington, so he moved his memorial to the other side of the state line.

While he may be an unknown in Goodland, he was quite popular in Burlington, even taking part in the annual high school homecoming parade. But instead of a float, he rode his own casket. You see, Gernhart had a thing about funerals. In 1951, when he was well into his seventies, he decided to throw his own, to ensure it was done right. At the time, he was fit to be tied that his relatives had skimped on his sister's funeral, so he planned his own ceremony complete with expensive casket, brass band, and prefuneral lunch.

At first, the folks of Burlington wanted nothing to do with Gernhart's harebrained scheme, but when he offered to pay good money to anyone willing to mourn, folks began lining up. That first funeral drew 1,000 bereaved citizens, more than half the population of the town at that time. Gernhart had so much fun that he decided to do it again the next year. And the next.

Eventually, *Life* magazine even ran a two-page spread about the thirty-some funerals that Garner threw for himself before finally dying in 1980 for real at the ripe old age of 105. By then, he'd worn out his casket, which prompted him to upgrade to the mausoleum.

Lions and Tigers and Zebras, Oh My!
Burlington

If you think a Bentley or a Lamborghini is an expensive ride, try out the Kit Carson County Carousel in Burlington. Each of the forty-six elaborately carved animals is worth a quarter million dollars. Add them together and you've got what may be the world's most costly form of transportation. It's certainly one of the most artistic.

Built in 1905, the antique carousel, one of Colorado's thirteen National Historic Landmarks, was the sixth of seventy-four carousels

Round and round on a genuine "quarter" horse.
Kit Carson County Carousel Association

made by the Philadelphia Toboggan Company. It has forty-five Victorian oil paintings and forty-six exquisitely detailed creatures, including a giraffe with a snake twined around its neck, a zebra with a gnome under its saddle blanket, deer with real antlers, and horses with real horses' tails and saddle trappings patterned after those used on

Watering Hole

With Dasani and Aquafina costing more than a gallon of gas, water connoisseurs may want to think about heading to Brush, Colorado, with empty jugs. This little town of just over 5,000 has its own well and water supply that is so pure it requires no chlorine. The H_2O coming out of Brush faucets is also naturally softened by the surrounding sand hills.

cavalry mounts in the eighteenth-century Napoleonic Wars. A fully restored 1912 Wurlitzer Monster Military Band Organ with 255 pipes, drums, and cymbals accompanies the animals with the sound of a fifteen-piece band.

Even though transportation like this is priceless, if you show up in Burlington between Memorial Day and Labor Day, you can catch a ride on the Kit Carson County Carousel for a mere 25 cents. It's located at the Carson Fairgrounds in Burlington. Call (800) 825-0208, or visit www.kitcarsoncountycarousel.com for more information.

Junkrassic Park

Cheraw

I'll spin you a tale about Junkrassic Park,
And how on this quest I became embarked.
For five or six years I've been at this game,
My biggest endeavor, my claim to fame.
—Johnnie Allen, "The Legacy"

In the early 1990s Johnnie Allen's wife asked him to duplicate a scrap metal rooster the couple had seen on a peach-picking excursion to the Western Slope. It was a moment that can be compared only to Georgia O'Keeffe's meeting Alfred Stieglitz.

★ ★

The "Duke"—Jon Way-In.
Junkrassic Park

As destiny tends to happen, Allen's rooster, a whimsical bird that he fashioned out of a saw blade and a mower cart, started him on what can only be described as a rampage of artistic achievement. He has since created eighty different sculptures, all made from farm

⋆ ⋆

implements, telephone poles, and other items plucked out of the junk heap.

There's a 15-foot Statue of Liberty, for example, with a head-dress made from an Oldsmobile hubcap and shoes that once were planter shields. Along with the Lady of Liberty, there's John L. Weigh (pun intended), Infidel Castro, Adolf Hitler, a P-38 airplane, the Eiffel Tower, and a 25- to 30-foot dinosaur that started life as a truck frame.

"All farmers have junk," explains Allen as to where he gets his art supplies. As for ideas: "They just come to me when I'm lying in bed."

The retired farmer's favorite sculpture is a 12-foot giraffe that he made out of a 50-gallon barrel and a grain auger. Each of the eighty sculptures has a clever name that Allen paints on a sign made of sheet metal, tin, or angle iron. When he's not sculpting, Allen writes books, draws cartoons, and plays guitar and piano in a western band called Jamboree.

Junkrassic Park can be viewed at 35574 CR JJ, Cheraw; if you want to call the father of eight and grandfather of some twenty grandkids, he can be reached at (719) 853-6519.

What a Long, Conventional Trip It's Been
Fort Morgan

Although you won't see tie-dye, madras skirts, and wiggle dances, there's a fan base that worships Glenn Miller much like Dead-heads venerate Jerry Garcia, but it's doubtful they'd appreciate the comparison.

Glenn Miller groupies congregate in Clarinda, Iowa (that's where their leader was born); at Twinwood Airfield in Bedfordshire, England (that's where his plane took off before he crash-dove into the Atlantic Ocean on December 15, 1944); and in Colorado's own Fort Morgan, where the popular big band leader graduated from Fort Morgan High.

Not only did the guy who received the music industry's first gold record play trombone for the Marching Maroons and start his first

★ ★

band at Fort Morgan High (it was called the Mick-Miller Melody Five), but he also played left end for the school's conference-winning football team and landed a football scholarship to the University of Colorado. The fact that he skipped his own graduation (his mother picked up his diploma) for a gig in Wyoming should have been the first clue that music, not football, was going to provide his destiny. In retrospect, playing graduation hooky was a wise choice.

At the time Johnnie Pumphandle (his classmates' nickname for him) attended high school in Fort Morgan, his constant trombone practicing was a tad bit annoying to teachers, students, and neighbors. Once, to find a secluded place to play, he and his brother climbed onto the roof of the school, where they were later arrested.

Now, however, Fort Morgan is proud of their favorite son, celebrating each summer with the Glenn Miller Swingfest, which draws Glenn Millerheads to Colorado for big band picnics, museum tours, champagne brunches, historical presentations, a dinner dance, and the Little Brown Jug Race. Tours are also given of Miller's old haunts, such as his three Fort Morgan homes, his parents' tombstones, and Western Sugar, where he once worked.

The Fort Morgan Museum at 414 Main Street (970-542-4010; www.ftmorganmus.org) has a Glenn Miller exhibit featuring old family photos, a copy of his 1941 recording "Chattanooga Choo Choo," a ticket he signed at his last civilian concert, and the flag that flew over the U.S. Capitol on the fiftieth anniversary of his 1944 disappearance over the English Channel.

Wonder Tower, Builds Bodies Six Ways
Genoa

P. T. Barnum had nothing on Charles W. Gregory, the railroad engineer and entrepreneur who in 1926 built the 60-foot Wonder Tower, a giant wooden sightseeing tower from which you supposedly can view six states. Standing at the top of the tower that looks an awful lot like a red-and-white lighthouse, Gregory would yell through

The tallest point between New York and Denver???
Jerry Chubbuck

a megaphone at passing cars. "How are things in the Sunflower State?" he'd boom out to cars with Kansas tags, or "You're a long way from home, Buckeyes" to cars with plates from Ohio.

Inside the Wonder Tower were imitation caverns, and since it stood next to a gas station, motel, and restaurant, it became an official Greyhound bus station and a popular truck stop. When Gregory died in 1942, the property fell into disrepair, and when I-70 found a better route in 1952, the motel, gas station, and restaurant disappeared.

The good news is the tower is still there, and, yes, old Charles W. Gregory would be proud. Not only has it been turned into a museum with a large collection of Native American artifacts and a weird variety of bottles, baseball mitts, and farm implements, most of which are hanging from the ceiling, but it also features an animal monstrosities exhibit complete with a two-headed calf, an eight-legged pig embryo, and an albino rattlesnake.

★ ★

Outside the vintage roadside attraction are swarms of cars, but don't be fooled. They're just rusted-out automobiles that make the place look like it's a popular destination. And all those people hanging out the windows at the top of the tower? Upon closer inspection, you'll discover they're really just water-warped two-by-fours wrapped in red fabric, stuffed with rags, and wearing straw hats.

Admission to the Wonder Tower is a mere $1, a veritable steal when you figure vintage postcards of the place sell on eBay for as high as $24.99. And if you're able to identify six items that Jerry Chubbuck, the current owner, calls his "Guess What?" quiz, he'll gladly refund your dollar. But don't get too eager, as items can range from rooster eyeglasses and camel nose bells to a walrus penis.

While the "see six states" claim is a bit of an exaggeration, the tower—which you can still climb—does provide westbound visitors with their very first sight of the Rocky Mountains.

To see the two-headed calf, the dummies, the rusted-out cars, or the six states, take exit 371 off I-70 onto CO 109, go 2 miles, and turn left on Frontage Road. The phone number is (719) 763-2309; the official address, 30121 Frontage Road, Genoa.

Rocky Mountain Low
Holly

In a state that claims fifty-four 14,000-footers, the country's highest municipal airport, and the country's highest incorporated town, it's no wonder that Holly often gets overlooked. Holly, which is located in the southeast corner of the state near the Kansas border, is Colorado's answer to that burning question: How low can you go?

Holly sits at the mouth of Wild Horse Creek and the Arkansas River, was once a stop on the Santa Fe Trail, and is the state's lowest point. But even with an elevation of only 3,387 feet, it's still the highest low point of any of the fifty states.

Holly is located on US 50, just minutes from Coolidge, Kansas.

✦ ✦

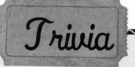

Trivia

In 1885 Trail City, aka "Hellhole on the Arkansas," straddled the Colorado/Kansas state line. Each of the town's forty-two rollicking saloons had a front door facing the Centennial State but a back door opening to Kansas. Fugitives when confronted with Colorado or Kansas lawmen had an easy escape hatch to a different state.

Tale of Four Cities

Julesburg

Julesburg, the county seat of Sedgwick County, is a moving company's worse nightmare. Here's the conversation I'm thinking of:

New home owner to the movers carrying in that weighty armoire: "Just set it over there by the window."

New home owner: "No, wait, I think it would probably look better in the west corner."

New home owner: "Except maybe we should try it over here by the couch."

Since Julesburg was established in 1859 as a French trading post, it has been moved a grand total of four times. When half-French, half-Indian Jules Beni modestly named his new trading post after himself, it was located about 1.5 miles southeast of Ovid. But on February 2, 1865, after a heated battle between the U.S. Army and a coalition of Cheyenne, Arapaho, and Sioux Indians, the town, with its telegraph office, blacksmith shop, stables, and billiards saloon, all made of rough-hewn logs, was burnt to the ground.

A year later, in 1866, Julesburg #2 was slapped together a couple miles east. Used mostly as a stagecoach stop, it was abandoned the next year when the Union Pacific laid railroad tracks several miles

★ ★

The Pony Express Station at Julesburg #1 claimed Buffalo Bill as one of its riders. Colorado Welcome Center at Julesburg

north. The folks of Julesburg picked up stakes and set up shop (Julesburg #3) close to the nearest station.

But then that dang indecisive Union Pacific decided to branch off to Denver and move the tracks again. Once more, Julesburg resurrected itself, moving several miles eastward, only this time residents decided to rename themselves Denver Junction. But that impostor name was short-lived: By 1881 it reverted to Julesburg (#4).

I'm happy to report Julesburg #4 has been there ever since. The schizophrenic town is located at the intersection of I-76 and US 385.

★ ★

Julesburg #1, a former Pony Express station, has an official marker on CR 28, a gravel road 1.5 miles southeast of Ovid.

Also at Julesburg #4: a statue of a Pony Express rider, even though the Julesburg Pony Express station, where Buffalo Bill was recruited to join the short-lived mail route, was located at Julesburg #1.

Heil, Kit Carson
Kit Carson

It's not news to anybody that J. Edgar Hoover was a suspicious man. But eleven years of probing into the possibility that Adolf Hitler might have faked his 1945 suicide and was living in the United States could possibly be termed extreme. Leads the former FBI director followed included a report of Hitler dining in a Washington restaurant in 1946, diving out of a New Orleans train in 1948, and being treated by a doctor in St. Louis for an intestinal disorder. Although Hitler's medical records did show intestinal problems, none of Hoover's leads panned out.

But the one connection that was 100 percent legit is the 8,960-acre ranch that the evil despot owned outside the Colorado town of Kit Carson. Of course, by the time of Hitler's "alleged fake suicide," the land had already reverted to the federal government.

Hitler, like many Europeans, had a huge fascination with cowboys and the U.S. West. While growing up, he read stories by Karl May, a German who penned riveting tales about America's cowboys and Indians. He even learned to throw a lasso.

When Hitler became the chancellor of Germany, he confiscated a $20,000 mortgage note from a German family, most likely Jewish, who had inherited the Colorado ranch from a relative in the United States. After the United States declared war on Germany, the government reclaimed his Kit Carson ranch and eventually sold it to a man from New Mexico. But if you look in the abstract listings in Cheyenne County, you'll see the German führer's name.

Adolf Hitler's former ranch is located 4 miles outside Kit Carson.

★ ★

I've Been through the Desert to a Fort with No Name
La Junta

Okay, so the 180-foot adobe fort that sat in the middle of nowhere during the 1830s and 1840s did have a name. But the name seemed to change every month or so. The fort that's now a National Historic Site and officially called Bent's Old Fort (not to be confused with Bent's New Fort, which was smaller and built 30 miles down the road) was also called Fort William, Fort Fauntleroy, Fort Wise, and "the castle in the desert" at one time or another. And it did seem like a castle to travelers along the Santa Fe Trail who hadn't seen anything but wide-open spaces for hundreds of miles. The Indian trading post, the only white settlement since Dodge City, had all the supplies a pioneer could ever need. You could even get Kit Carson's autograph if

Last I heard, it was called Bent's Old Fort, but that was two days ago. National Park Service

★ ★

you happened to be there at the right time. The famous hunter called Bent's Fort home for a spell in the 1840s.

The multinamed fort was built in 1833 by William Bent, his brother Charles, and Ceran St. Vrain, who together started one of the most successful Indian trading operations in the West. The private trading post had walls that were 4 feet thick and had cactus planted on top to discourage climbers.

According to one story, William Bent, after trying to sell the fort to federal government officials (they did rent it for a staging area during the Mexican War), got pissed when they wouldn't offer a fair price and blew the place up in 1859. It was completely rebuilt (as close to the original as possible) in 1976 and today offers tours and living history programs.

Bent's Old Fort National Historic Site is located on CO 194, 6 miles east of La Junta. Take US 50 out of La Junta and follow the signs. The phone number is (719) 383-5010; or visit www.nps.gov/beol/.

Dance Fever
La Junta

Ask any junior high girl: It's next to impossible to get a junior high boy to dance. But not in La Junta, where junior high and high school boys have been dancing, gliding, leaping, and whirling for going on seventy-five years.

Granted, there aren't exactly girls involved, and their dancing is not your typical gymnasium variety. Rather, the Koshare Indian Dancers belong to Boy Scout Troop 232, and their dances are historic reenactments of the war dances and ceremonial rituals of the Plains and Pueblo Indians who once lived in the area. The world-famous troupe performs between fifty and sixty shows a year.

Started in 1933 by scoutmaster James Francis "Buck" Burshears, the Koshare Indian Dancers have also built a world-class museum that not only features the world's largest self-supporting log roof, but also has one of the country's best collections of Native American art.

Great uniform, but where do you put the badges?
Koshare Indian Museum

The dancers, with bodies emblazoned in bold black-and-white stripes, give a show every summer Saturday at the museum. They make their own regalia and drums and claim to have more Eagle Scouts than any troop in the United States.

To see the dancing Boy Scouts, visit the Koshare Indian Museum off US 50 on the campus of Otero Junior College. The phone number is (719) 384-4411 or (800) 693-5482; street address is 115 West Eighteenth Street; and Web site is www.koshare.org.

* *

Grauman's Chinese Theatre for Dinosaurs
South of La Junta, Picketwire Canyonlands (Comanche National Grassland)

Unlike Tom Cruise and Susan Sarandon and everyone else who left their foot- and handprints at Grauman's Chinese Theatre, the dinosaurs who left their prints in Purgatoire Valley weren't celebrities. Or at least the archaeologists who first reported them in *Life* magazine in 1935 didn't ask for autographs.

All we do know is there are 1,300 dinosaur prints in a ¼-mile swath on the west end of Picketwire Canyonlands. It's the longest mapped site of dinosaur tracks in North America. Forty percent of the footprints were left by brontosaurs who were trolling the shores of a lake for algae, clams, snails, and fish. The other 60 percent were left by packs of allosaurus—ferocious three-toed, meat-eating scavengers. The site is the largest of the thirty known Morrison (150 million-year-old) dinosaur formations, containing more footprints than all the others combined.

The footprints are located roughly 35 miles south of La Junta in the Picketwire Canyonlands, which were added to the Comanche National Grassland in 1991. Call (719) 384-2181 for more information; www.vipgrafx.com/misc/cng1.htm.

That's One Way to Sell a Used Car
Lamar

I've heard of some pretty outrageous gimmicks for selling used cars, but Stagner Inc. in Lamar might just win the prize. Potential customers may think they're coming to see a 175 million-year-old gas station, but they end up falling in love with the 1988 Ford Fairlane that's sitting on the adjacent lot.

The gas station is no longer in operation; in fact, it isn't really 175 million years old. But the wood that it's made of is at least that old—it has been petrified for millions of years. When it was constructed in 1932 out of petrified trees, some of which are 4 feet in diameter and weigh 3,200 pounds, lumber dealer W. G. Brown figured a gas

★ ★

I've heard of hardwood floors, but hardwood walls?
Territorial Magazine

station made out of wood that can't burn and can't deteriorate ought to bring in a tourist or two. One of those tourists was Robert Ripley, whose "Believe It or Not" column made him the first cartoon millionaire. Sure enough, Ripley wrote about the unusual gas station and put it on the map.

In 1962 the Petrified Service Station was sold to Lamar Tire Service, which used it to sell tires (and the occasional used car) until it grew right out of the building with the world's oldest hardwood floors. It's currently owned by Stagner Inc. (the 20,000-square-foot operation is right next door), and you'll still see camera-toting tourists who snap pictures of themselves in front of the old building with the wood that turned to stone.

Stagner Inc., which technically conducts business out of the old building at 501 Main Street, is right off the intersection of US 50 and US 287. Phone (719) 336-3462.

* *

Redder than a Navajo Blanket

Lamar

Tom Mix, the star of more than 300 Westerns, liked to embellish the truth. His boss at the famous 101 Wild West Show used to say, "Tom could color a story redder than a Navajo blanket." He used to tell the ladies (this was in between his three wives) and anybody else who'd listen that he'd ridden with Teddy Roosevelt in the charge up San Juan Hill, that he served in the Boxer Rebellion in China, and that he was a decorated Texas Ranger.

Once when being interviewed in Denver, Mix told the reporter that before heading to Hollywood, he served as high sheriff of Two Buttes, a small town near Lamar. When the reporter, apparently more interested in veracity than the fancy stunt rider was, pointed out that there was no such thing as a "high sheriff" in this country, Mix changed his story. "Well, I was the 'undersheriff of Prowers County' then," he revised.

Truth is, Tom Mix was a bartender in Lamar. He mixed drinks for George Yowell's saloon in 1906.

Twice Is Not Enough

Springfield

If you think MOMA has limited hours, you should try the art gallery at Crack Cave. Well, to call it a gallery is a bit of a stretch. It's more like a . . . well, it's a cave, but a cave etched with hundreds of ancient pictographs at least a thousand years old. The reason the hours are so scanty is because the drawings are illuminated only at sunrise, and only two sunrises a year at that. The clever artists who left the etchings designed them so they are viewable only on the vernal and autumnal equinoxes. That means the gallery is "open" for biz only on March 21 or 22 and on September 21 or 22.

On both those days, the sun seeps onto the cave wall, making a shadow that points like a sundial to the Celtic-style markings. It points to them one at a time, moving across the north wall of the cave until all the markings are aglow. The solar show lasts all of eight to twelve minutes. Some researchers insist the writings on Crack Cave are in Ogham, an ancient Celtic language. Others claim early Indians left them.

Nobody is in disagreement that those two days are good ones to throw a festival, which Springfield, the nearest town, does each spring and fall equinox. For more info, call the Springfield Chamber of Commerce at (719) 523-4061, or visit their Web site at www.springfieldco .info.

Crack Cave is located in Picture Canyon, which is in the Comanche National Grassland. Other rock art in Picture Canyon are individual figures such as the "Spotted Woman," "Black Buffalo," "Blue Horse," "Warrior with Two Spears," and a stone that scholars have linked to ancient birthing ceremonies.

Raising the Dead
Sterling

Twenty years ago Bradford Rhea didn't have enough money to pursue his real dream: sculpting in marble. So he settled for the only thing he could afford—dead trees that the town of Sterling had earmarked for removal.

At the time, he was working as a lab technician at the local hospital. He approached city big cheese with the following offer: "Not only can I save you the cost of removing those old trees, but I'll bring them back to life." Now that's an offer a city can't afford to refuse. Before long, Rhea had turned eleven dead trees into living tree sculptures. A dying elm in Columbine Park, for example, became a herd of giraffes gazing at the stars. Another diseased elm in front of Burger King became a whimsical depiction of the hamburger chain's characters. A farmer's hundred-year-old cottonwood tree turned into *Seraphim,* an intricate depiction of a lion, a bull, an eagle, and other creatures from Revelations 4:6.

And Sterling, a town that tends to get dwarfed next to Colorado's famous mountain towns, was suddenly thrust into the national spotlight.

This herd of giraffes used to be an elm tree.
Northeast Colorado Travel Region

★ ★

Visitors started showing up to gawk at the amazing sculptures, and in 1993, when Pope John Paul II visited the United States, the State Department called Rhea and asked him to sculpt a walking stick for President Bill Clinton to give to his Holy Visitor. Rhea had exactly seven days to sculpt the staff from an aged honey locust tree, a considerable rush when you figure his other sculptures can take as long as 2,500 hours to complete.

Rhea eventually got so famous (he was dubbed the Michelangelo of the Plains) that he was able to move from dead trees to marble. In fact, when some of his living tree sculptures started rotting, the city of Sterling came up with the money to recast them in bronze—but not before trying linseed oil, tung oil, and canned foam that was squirted into the center where the rotting wood had been removed. After all, those trees were nearly as famous—at least in eastern Colorado—as Michelangelo's *David.*

Although a few of the living trees are still trees (*Seraphim,* the cottonwood mentioned earlier, and *Wind Lace,* to name a couple, can be viewed at the Sterling Public Library), many of Rhea's works are now bronze. You can pick up a map at the visitor center (*Metamorphosis,* a bronze formerly known as a tree, sits out front) at 109 North Front Street; phone (866) 522-5070. Brad's Web site is www.thesculptor.net.

Shrine On, Harvest Moon
Trinidad

The seventy-bed Mt. San Rafael Hospital in Trinidad has several notable distinctions, not least of them being that Dr. Stanley Biber performed more than 3,800 sex change operations there, making Trinidad the "sex change capital of the world."

But the distinction I'd rather tell you about is the Ave Maria Shrine that's located on the hillside south of the notorious hospital. It's a tiny white stucco building with an even tinier cross on top. It was built in 1961 on the exact spot where fifty-three years earlier the Virgin Mary appeared to Dr. John Espy.

★ ★

Although history is a bit vague on all the details, the story goes something like this: Espy was caught on his horse in a horrible blizzard. He feared for his life. Just when he was about to despair, to lie down and die, he noticed a glowing light just outside Trinidad, although he didn't recognize it as Trinidad at the time since visibility in the blizzard was all of 2 inches. The light, as the story has it, turned out to be a glowing statue of the Virgin.

Since Mary doesn't show up just anywhere, locals decided it would be a good place to build a shrine, although the Virgin Mary that inhabits the place now is a statue from France.

The Ave Maria Shrine is located just behind the hospital that was started by Carmelite nuns at 410 Benedicta Avenue.

Without Fanfare

Wild Horse

Hard to believe a town with only 538 people would be the birthplace of celebrity fan clubs. But a 9,000-acre wheat farm in Wild Horse, Colorado, is where fan clubs got their start. Loretta, Loudilla, and Kay Johnson, three sisters who grew up on the farm, started a Loretta Lynn fan club back in 1963. They took turns being president, vice president, and secretary/treasurer.

Their Loretta Lynn fan club became so successful that other country artists began flocking to them for advice. The unassuming sisters even began hosting a popular fan-sponsored country show in Nashville where fans got the chance to meet and get autographs from their favorite country stars. Loretta Lynn herself suggested the sisters use their expertise to start an umbrella organization for fan clubs, which they did in 1967. Their outfit, the International Fan Club Organization, not only has an impressive Web site (www.ifco.org) with a database of literally hundreds of fan clubs, but it also has become the clearinghouse for fan clubs and a watchdog for the industry.

Before long, the Johnson sisters became celebrities themselves, even luring famed photographer Richard Avedon to Wild Horse to shoot the founders of the IFCO. And like many good country celebrities, they picked up and moved to Nashville.

The Things We'll Do for Love
Wray

For four weekends in late March/early April, tourists flock to tiny Wray, Colorado, so they can get up at 4 a.m. to watch a bizarre mating ritual. No, they're not Larry Flynt devotees; rather, they're Audubon types who get their jollies watching greater prairie chickens puff up their orange throat sacs, fan out their tails, stamp their feet, and strut around like John Travolta in *Saturday Night Fever.*

The mating tours of the greater prairie chicken (not to be confused with the lesser prairie chicken) are sponsored by the East Yuma County Historical Society, and lest "the dawn's early light" sounds too early for a tour, just know these popular tours sell out weeks in advance. After all, it's not just anywhere you can see male prairie chickens hopping, sprinting, spinning in circles, and facing off with eerie mating calls that sound a little bit like air being blown across a Coke bottle. The lady prairie chickens find it irresistible.

The one-of-a-kind tours take place at Kitzmiller Ranch and include a Friday night presentation at the Wray museum, a cookout, and a giant ranch-style breakfast. The prairie chickens' leks (mating arenas) are located along CR 45, 11 miles north of Wray. To get your very own button with the slogan "I got up with the prairie chickens," call (970) 332-3484, or visit www.wraychamber.net.

The Corniest

Oscar Hammerstein got it all wrong in his well-known song from *South Pacific,* "A Wonderful Guy." The line goes like this: "I'm as corny as Kansas in August / High as a flag on the Fourth of July." Well, turns out the county that produces the most corn in the entire United States is not in Kansas, but in Colorado. Yuma County, of which Wray is the county seat, holds the record for producing more corn than any other U.S. county thanks to irrigation from the Ogallala aquifer. Unfortunately, "I'm as corny as Colorado in August" just didn't have the right beat.

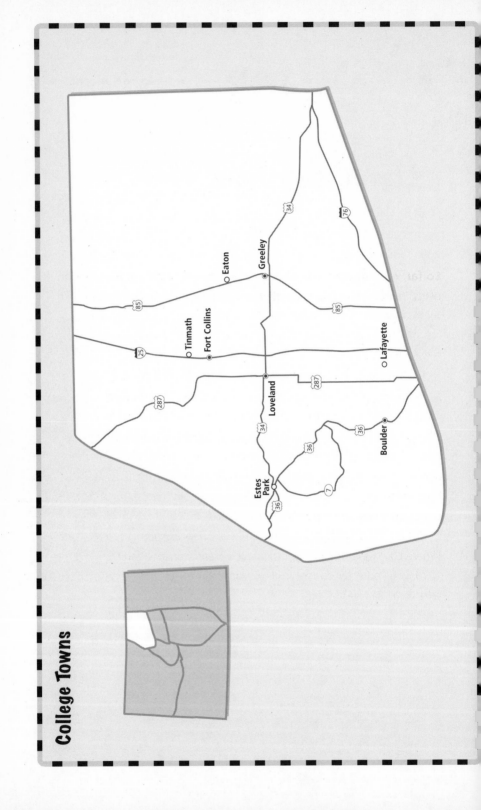

College Towns

2

College Towns

So far, my daughter, who is only fifteen, hasn't discussed her college plans, but if she so much as mentions Boulder, Fort Collins, Greeley, or, for that matter, any other Colorado college town as potential beneficiaries of her above-average brain, I have to admit I'll be deeply torn. I'm her mother, after all.

On one hand, I'd be worried. How could she possibly concentrate on physics and nuclear science when there's a contortionist nearby who can squeeze himself into a 20-inch Plexiglas cube? How could she possibly get her papers written and her tests studied for when there's the Antique Washing Machine Museum only thirty minutes away? For that matter, how could she ever pull herself away long enough to attend class when there's a guy in town who makes giant dinosaurs and Puff the Magic Dragons out of farm machinery?

But on the other hand, where could she possibly have so much fun? Where could she possibly get this much creative inspiration?

Maybe I'd better put the college applications I ordered last week out where she can see them.

★ ★

Nanu-Nanu
Boulder

First, I'd like to apologize to the residents of a certain house on Pine Street in Boulder. I know that the last thing you need is more gawkers coming by to peep in your windows. Just because the exterior of your lovely Victorian home was filmed as the residence of *Mork and Mindy*, the famous Orkian and his wife who starred on the hit TV series of the late '70s/early '80s, doesn't mean you deserve a constant stream of tourists posing for photos in front of your house.

So listen up, earthlings. Yes, the home is still there in all its glory, but the interior is nothing like the set where Robin Williams and Pam Dawber carried on their antics. The fence, the view-blocking tall fence, is there for a reason, and the Pearl Street Mall and the Boulderado Hotel, both which are mere blocks away, are 100 percent more interesting.

The Mork and Mindy House is located at 1619 Pine Street. But don't tell them I told you.

Cursed Again

According to local legend, an Arapaho Amerindian named Chief Niwot put a curse on the Boulder Valley in 1858 when the white man first showed up. The curse is translated a couple different ways. Take your pick.

"People seeing the beauty of this valley will want to stay, and their staying will be the undoing of the beauty." Or "Once you gaze upon the beauty of the Flatirons, you will never be happy anywhere else."

* *

Flesh! It's What's for Dinner
Boulder

At one time there were two cafeterias in the country named after
Alferd Packer, the only man in America ever to be convicted of cannibalism. But the Alferd E. Packer Cafeteria in Washington, D.C. (it
was the lunchroom for the Department of Agriculture), eventually got
shut down. The General Services Administration, which paid the bills,
deemed the name in poor taste and took down the bronze plaque
that immortalized the hungry Coloradoan.

The other Alferd E. Packer Memorial Grill, I'm happy to report, is
alive and thriving. In fact, this restaurant, on the main floor of the
Memorial Center at the University of Colorado in Boulder, even sells
Alferd hats and T-shirts with the logo "Have a Friend for Lunch."

Of course, Alferd Packer is what you might call a celebrity in the
Centennial State, with statues, songs, and cannibal collectible dolls

El Canibal is one heck of a burrito!
University of Colorado, Boulder

★ ★

named in his honor. Trey Parker, the University of Colorado student who went on to cocreate *South Park,* even wrote a cheesy horror comedy about Colorado's favorite son. Started as a project for an advanced film class, *Cannibal: The Musical* is available on DVD.

In 1874 Alferd Packer (his real name was Alfred, but a tattoo artist made a mistake, and the misspelling, well, stuck) advertised himself as a guide for leading would-be prospectors through the treacherous Rocky Mountains. On his last excursion, his sense of direction was intact, but his timing was off. He and five clients got stranded in a blizzard. When rations ran thin, Alferd, being the pragmatic sort, killed his clients, stashed them in a snowdrift, and used them as munchies until the spring thaw arrived.

Since territorial law frowned on such practicality, Alferd was arrested and tried for murder, though supporters claimed his sentence was swayed by political posturing. When Judge Melville B. Gerry found him guilty, he said, "There was only six Democrats in all of Hinsdale County, and you 'et five of 'em." Although he was sentenced to "hang by the neck until you are dead, dead, dead" (those were Judge Gerry's exact words) and did spend several years in a prison in Cañon City, he was eventually released on a technicality, became a vegetarian, and made a modest living selling autographed photos of himself.

The Alferd E. Packer Memorial Grill—where, among other things, you can buy an El Canibal, a giant burrito, and see a marble bust of Packer—is located directly below the Glenn Miller Lounge in the Memorial Center at CU.

Thinking Inside the Box
Boulder

Lots of folks feel squeezed at work—by their bosses, their deadlines, their overflowing inboxes. But nobody gets the pressure like Ibashi-I, a Boulder street performer, who, during his fifteen-minute performance, squeezes himself into a clear, 20-inch-square Plexiglas cube.

The human pretzel doing his thing. Downtown Boulder

If you need to throw him into a category, contortionist would work, but the St. Kitts native who has been performing for at least ten years calls what he does "Rasta yoga." He's able to stretch and bend himself into positions that the rest of us clearly know are "impossible." The father of three started performing thirty-five years ago in the Caribbean and says that he taught himself everything he knows.

Not that you could ever miss a fellow who bends himself in half and slides through a plastic cylinder, but Mitford Ibashi-I Brown is the Rasta-looking guy in the black tights with the rainbow-colored gym shorts. He's often yelling, "Hey everybody, look at me!"

He's usually on Pearl Street Mall, Boulder's 4-block pedestrian mall, seven days a week.

Let's Do the Twist
Boulder

If you're one of the 50,000 runners who compete every year in the Bolder Boulder, a world-famous road race with a 10K course of

His work is full of hot air.
Downtown Boulder

nonstop live music and entertainment, you probably already know Bongo, the Balloon-o-Matic. He's the guy who plays the drums for the Folsom Street Belly Dancers, the one with the thick blond beard and the ponytail. Or if you've been to Boulder's annual "Lucky" parade, you've seen Bongo leading the parade with his Blue Balloon Band.

But if you're in Boulder on one of the ordinary days (not that any day in Boulder could ever rate as ordinary), you'll usually find Bongo on Pearl Street Mall turning biodegradable balloons into dinosaurs, dolphins, flowers, and hats. (Not surprisingly, before he was a professional balloon twister, Bongo worked for a singing telegram company.)

22222, 44444, 55555, and Other Amazing Zip Codes
Boulder

If you're like most people, you have no clue that 22222 is the zip code of Arlington, Virginia, that 44444 is the zip for mail carriers in Newton Falls, Ohio, or that Schenectady, New York, has the easy-to-remember zip code of 12345.

But if you're David Rosdeitcher, a street performer from Boulder, you know those three zip codes by heart, plus 48,000 more. Furthermore, you make your living by wowing people with your impressive command of the code of zip (which, as David can tell you, stands for zoning improvement plan).

Rosdeitcher took up memorizing zip codes in 1991 after a juggling career took him to hundreds of cities around the country. Not only can he identify tens of thousands of towns by their five-digit zip codes, but he also knows the landmarks and a popular restaurant in each locale. Plus, he can juggle seven balls or five clubs, all at the same time. For Rosdeitcher's finale, he forms a map of the United States from a yellow chain, assembles audience members onto the map, then tells an improvised story using each person and their hometown.

★ ★

Rosdeitcher started street performing in 1985 in New Orleans' French Quarter while getting an anthropology degree at Tulane University. He has performed at Epcot and holds the Guinness World Record for most zip codes recited in one sitting. During the off-season (winter in the case of street performers), he visits a new country every year.

A reporter once asked him why he doesn't put his unique talent to better use. "What better use is there than making people laugh?" was Rosdeitcher's reply.

To challenge the zip code man, find him standing on the black traffic barriers at Thirteenth and Pearl Streets.

Mintus Maximus
Boulder

A 30-by-40-foot sealed room in Boulder may be the best place in the universe to get rid of a cold. One hundred thousand pounds of dried peppermint, spearmint, and catnip, all waiting for their turn to debut in a hot cup of Celestial Seasonings tea, emit so much menthol that sinuses clear upon contact. In fact, the reason the famous so-called Mint Room is tightly sealed when guests aren't gawking is because it used to leach into the other botanicals. Rumor has it that without the seal, you can smell it a mile away. This Boulder company, known for its whimsical, colorful boxes and philosophical quotes, gives daily tours and even sells T-shirts, "I survived the Mint Room." Hairnets and beard nets, required when the factory is in production, are supplied. And if you don't get your fill of tea on the tour, a virtual impossibility since most of the company's 104 teas, 12 of which contain mint, are offered free before and after in the tearoom, you can sip even more at Boulder's ornate, hand-carved, hand-painted teahouse—a traditional Tajik *choihona*—a gift from it's sister city, Dushanbe, the capital of Tajikistan. Celestial Seasonings, 4600 Sleepytime Drive; (303) 581-1202; www.celestialseasonings.com.

Not a T-shirt, but a T-dress (made of tea bags).
Carol Keller

Can You Say "Yeehaw"?

Boulder

John Georgis isn't exactly sure why people started hollering "It's Banjo Billy!" at the top of their lungs every time they spotted his Boulder tour bus. After all, they don't yell "Hey, it's a taxi!" when a cab drives by or "Look, there's a limousine!" when a long black car with tinted windows whizzes by. But loudly acknowledging Banjo Billy's bus has become a Boulder tradition, one that Georgis's customers,

The only way to fly in Boulder.
John Georgis

twenty-eight when the tours are sold out, are required to answer with a hearty "Yeehaw!" One customer on each of the twice-daily tours even gets a megaphone and a job as "designated heckler."

But that's just part of the fun of Banjo Billy's Bus Tour, a wacky ninety-minute ride that takes tourists past Boulder's most infamous and little-known hot spots. Guests on the Banjo Billy bus—a refitted 1994 school bus that Georgis bought off eBay and drove to Boulder from Moline, Illinois, after offering to pick up every hitchhiker along the way—have a wide choice of seats. They can choose between several colors of Lazy-Boys, one of six saddles, or the comfy, over-stuffed couch in the back. Although Georgis's dream of turning the bus into a roving log cabin didn't quite pan out (the logs were too heavy to attach to the side of the bus), he was able to add a bunch of faux log fencing (it's lighter weight and scads cheaper), cut off the original roof, and weld a pitched roof that can be removed whenever the weather cooperates. Needless to say, he also added thirteen disco balls and a horn that "moos" like a cow.

Although the nine stops are the same (each guest, for example, hears about the false Boulder gold rush, a haunted hotel with three suicides and only one suicide note, and the obsessive forty-six-year-old Eagle Scout [see the "Man in Uniform" entry that follows] whose merit badge sash mysteriously shows up all over town), each tour is different. Sometimes incredibly different, like the time Georgis's tour included twelve drunk schoolteachers, a prim and proper elderly couple, and a Muslim family of six. But that's another story.

For more info on Banjo Billy's Bus Tours, call (720) 771-0087, or check out the Web site at www.banjobilly.com.

Man in Uniform
Boulder

It's one thing to honor God and country, but Boulder resident Clinton Dumm may have gotten a bit carried away with his responsibility as an Eagle Scout. For one thing, the uniform-happy outcast wore his merit badge sash over his business suit long after he parted ways with the noble organization. And when he died in 1970, he willed his home and all his belongings to Boy Scout Troop 71, a troop he didn't even join until he was thirty-six, a bit old for your average Cub Scout.

By the time he was forty-six, Dumm had earned his Eagle Scout rank, probably his life's proudest moment. But like many proud moments, it was followed by a disastrous fall. The scouting organization decided it was time for the single man who still lived with his mother to graduate. He was kicked out of the very organization he so revered.

And that's when the story gets weird. The scout leader of Troop 71 who inherited Dumm's house (besides the well-loved merit badge sash, the house contained a race car Dumm built in the basement that had to be taken apart to be removed) took the boxes and boxes of scouting memorabilia to his own home. Soon thereafter, the lights started flickering on their own, furniture started moving mysteriously around the house, and the infamous sash kept showing up, folded neatly, on the bed. The scoutmaster, who liked merit badge sashes, but not when they popped out of nowhere, eventually bequeathed Dumm's scouting belongings to the Boulder History Museum. And sure enough, the museum's lights started flickering, and it's rumored that a young man often answers the museum's phone . . . even when no one is there.

Dumm's childhood home, the one with the race car in the basement, was located at Marine and Sixth Streets. The Boulder History Museum is at 1206 Euclid Avenue on "The Hill"; phone (303) 339-3464; www.boulderhistorymuseum.org.

Good, Clean Fun
Eaton

Even though his wife, Barbara, thinks he should collect something lighter (she's the one who has to help him carry them), Lee Maxwell owns 1,155 antique washing machines, all of which have been restored to their original glory. Needless to say, an impressive, albeit heavy, collection like that is sure to have landed a coveted spot in the *Guinness Book of World Records,* which it did in 2000.

For years, Lee and Barbara spent every spring and fall scouring the country for old and unusual washing machines. "We looked like a traveling junkyard," says Lee about their motor home with the old trailer attached.

But now, Lee stays close to his priceless collection, which he dismantles, cleans, paints, and reassembles. He has antique washing machines that range from an early 1900s model that had a butter churn and meat grinder attachment to ninety old machines that were loaded onto a 48-by-8-foot semi by a hydraulic pig loader before they were toted from Tipp City, Ohio, to Colorado.

"After I retired, I needed a hobby. I don't play golf, and I'm not so

★ ★

No ring around the collar in this museum.
Lee Maxwell

good at bungee jumping, so I went for washing machines," he says.

Since there's no "blue book" for washing machines, and not exactly a huge market for collectors, Maxwell contents himself to keep all his washing machines and has opened what he calls a "hobby museum" in a shed behind his house. There aren't regular hours (you have to call ahead), and not just anybody can appreciate it. Lee has also written a 137-page book, *Save Women's Lives: The First Ever History of Washing Machines,* and he's currently working on a documentary.

To experience some of this good, clean fun, visit the Antique Washing Machine Museum at 35901 Weld CR 31, Eaton. Call ahead, since it's open by appointment only, (970) 454-1856; www.oldewash .com.

★ ★

Man on Wire

In 1974 a wire strung high across El Dorado Canyon was unceremoniously taken down. The powers that be were worried that some drunk CU frat boy might decide to do something stupid. Never mind that the reason the 635-foot tightrope was there in the first place was because Ivy Baldwin, an El Dorado resident and one of America's first hot balloonists, had already done something stupid, more than eighty-six times. Baldwin, a former circus performer, would cross the tightrope suspended 582 feet above the canyon floor to entertain guests of El Dorado's elite resorts. The last of the eighty-six crossings was in 1948 when Baldwin was eighty-two.

Key to My Heart
Estes Park

I suppose having the world's largest key collection was inevitable when Gordon and Ethel Mace decided to name their Estes Park inn after a best-selling mystery novel called *Seven Keys to Baldpate.*

As a gimmick, the couple gave each guest to the Baldpate Inn their own personal key. Guests kept the key—even after they checked out. During World War I, when metal was scarce and costs prohibitive, the Maces were forced to discontinue the practice that was inspired by the mystery novel written by Earl Derr Biggers, the same guy who created Charlie Chan. Loyal guests who returned year after year missed the tradition so much that they began bringing keys with them. And the competition became fierce: Who could bring the most exotic and farthest-flung key?

Today the collection—the world's largest, according to the Web site—has 20,000 keys, including ones to the Pentagon, Westminster Abbey, Mozart's wine cellar, Hitler's desk at the Berchtesgaden bomb shelter, and Frankenstein's castle, all of which are hanging in the room known as "The Key Room." Interestingly enough, the front door to the inn itself has no key.

Some of the famous names who have walked through the Baldpate Inn's keyless door over the years are Mae West, Jack Dempsey, Betty Grable, and Gregory Peck. It is also rumored that Ethel and Gordon are still around, haunting the historic inn they built on their homesteaded property in 1917.

To visit the twelve-room inn that now operates as a B&B, take CO 7 south from Estes Park. The address is 4900 South Highway 7; phone (970) 586-6151; www.baldpateinn.com.

Heeeere's Stanley

Estes Park

When Stanley Kubrick filmed *The Shining* with Jack Nicholson, he annoyed Stephen King, who wrote the novel, by not using the hotel that originally inspired the book. Maybe that's why King came back to The Stanley, the historic hotel in Estes Park, to film the TV miniseries.

The Stanley's venerable place in horror filmdom all started in the summer of 1974, when King and his wife, Tabitha, moved from Maine to Boulder. Needing a break from the kids that October, the Kings checked into Room 217 of the grand hotel that's less than 6 miles from Rocky Mountain National Park.

Built in 1909 by F. O. Stanley, the guy who invented the steam-driven automobile called the Stanley Steamer (not to be confused with the San Diego carpet cleaning business, which is spelled with two *E*'s), the old hotel inspired King to write his third novel, *The Shining,* about a winter hotel caretaker who goes insane from seeing ghosts.

According to the daily haunted hotel tours, King's character is not the only one to have seen ghosts. In fact, the entire fourth floor (once the servants' quarters) of The Stanley is allegedly filled with the sounds of children running and laughing through the halls. King supposedly heard a child calling out for his nanny. It's also reported that

★ ★

the ghosts of F. O. and Flora Stanley and Lord Dunraven, from whom they bought the land, also haunt the hotel.

Seventy-five percent of hotel staff report having seen or heard something otherworldly: lights flickering on and off, doors opening and closing by themselves, rooms mysteriously getting tidied up, a big loot of items reported lost turning up in Room 203, or strange "sit prints" on newly made beds. The supernatural activity usually heats up during a full moon.

Once the antique elevator came off its hinges, threatening to crash down the shaft; two staff members standing nearby were able to save it. And registration desk staff and guests sometimes hear the piano in the music room playing by itself.

So how dare Stanley Kubrick use the Timberline Lodge on Mount Hood in Oregon for the Overlook Hotel? What's worse is the interior shots were all done at EMI-Elstree Studios near London. As it turns out, Kubrick, a fanatical perfectionist, had nearly crashed his plane and decided that if he could make such a near-fatal mistake, there was no way he was getting on a plane that someone else was flying. Thus, the movie was shot on a soundstage in London.

To see the ghosts of F. O. and Flora, check out The Stanley at 333 Wonderview Avenue. Phone (970) 586-3371 or (800) 976-1377; www.stanleyhotel.com.

Kill Me Kate
Greeley

There's no quibbling with the fact that Albuquerque's American International Rattlesnake Museum has a pretty impressive collection of rattlesnake memorabilia. They've got musical instruments made from rattlesnake rattlers. They've got toys and games, ceramic, and glassware and even jewelry inspired by the deadly pit viper that comes in thirty different species. But in Greeley, at the Greeley History Museum, there's a rattlesnake flapper dress that those wannabes down in New Mexico would give their last and longest poisonous

Snake it to me, baby.
Carol Keller

fang for. Not only is the Greeley flapper dress made from the skins of fifty deadly rattlesnakes, but it was sewn by the very woman who shot them all.

Kate Slaughterbach became an international celebrity on October 28, 1925, when she shot and pummeled 140 rattlesnakes to death in a few short hours. It seems Kate and her three-year-old son, Ernie, had ridden down to a pond near Platteville, a little burg south of Greeley. When Kate dismounted to open the gate, the first rattler struck, a strategic mistake if ever there was one. Kate, a dirt farmer, happened to be a sharpshooter, and she wasted no time making quick work of that big boy. The racket, however, brought out a whole tribe of rattlers, which Kate strategically picked off one by one until her ammo began to run dry. Luckily for Kate and for Ernie, she spotted a NO HUNTING sign, which she used to clobber the rest of her 140 victims.

Even though this was before YouTube, where anyone can become an overnight celebrity, Kate's neighbor alerted a reporter to her heroic feat, and the word quickly spread around the world. Kate not only

★ ★

used fifty of the skins, which filled three bathtubs when she hauled them home, to make the lusted-after dress, but she also made a pair of shoes and a necklace, all of which she wore regularly to local functions.

Rattlesnake Kate's old farmhouse was moved from Platteville to Greeley's Centennial Village in 2002, and the dress, which is hermetically sealed in its own special case, compliments of the Shawsheen Questers, can be admired at the Greeley History Museum. Kate's gravestone, laid forty-four years later than it would have been had she not been such a dead ringer, resides in the Mizpah Cemetery in Platteville.

The Greeley History Museum is at 714 Eighth Street; (970) 350-9220; www.greeleygov.com.

Diamonds Are a State's Best Friend
Kelsey Lake

Diamonds may be forever, but they're certainly on again/off again in Colorado, where the country's only diamond mine opens, then closes, then opens again. The Kelsey Lake Diamond Mine, located northwest of Fort Collins on the Wyoming border, has produced some impressive gemstones over the years, including North America's largest-known cut diamond, a pale yellow 16.86-karat faceted stone found in 1997, and a 28.3-karat yellow diamond that, when cut and polished, weighed in at 5.4 karats and sold for $87,500. It's estimated that hidden beneath Kelsey Lake's eight veins of kimberlite ore are between 60,000 and 250,000 karats of diamonds. But at 8,000 feet they're expensive to mine, and local environmentalists have put up their fists, claiming open-pit diamond mining produces the largest waste-rock-to-product ratios of any commodity.

Still, the diamond trade is a $6 billion a year industry, and after being tarnished (*Blood Diamond*, anyone?) by revelations that African rebel groups use proceeds from diamond sales to commit atrocities against elected governments, Colorado Diamonds, now a trademarked name, might just have a leg up on the only other place in the United States with diamonds—a state park in Arkansas.

★ ★

The first company to mine Kelsey Lake unearthed, in less than three years, more than 1,000 karats of diamonds before going bankrupt in 1999. The next company found one hundred small diamonds overlooked by the first company when they moved some old crushing equipment on the first day. Still, they shuttered their operations in April 2002.

But hope springs eternal. In 2008 DiamonEx Ltd., a junior diamond explorer that made headlines with finds in Botswana, filed papers to explore the region once again.

The twenty-plus acres of diamond-producing kimberlite pipes are located in Larimer County along the Wyoming border.

Before Buffy

Lafayette

Since official records from 1918 are scanty, it's hard to verify with complete accuracy that (1) Fodor Glava is even buried in the plot he bought in the Lafayette Municipal Cemetery and that (2) Mr. Glava was indeed a vampire. But don't tell locals you suspect foul play.

After all, they've been daring one another to stand near the vampire's grave for nearly ninety years. A good number of them report having seen a tall, thin man with a black coat, dark hair, and long fingernails sitting on top of the stone. People show up on Halloween to take photos. Even a former chief of police said he found a doll with a pin stuck through its heart on top of the grave.

According to the persistent myth, the tree growing from the middle of the grave (right where the vampire's heart would presumably be) sprouted from the stake that killed him. The unruly red rose bushes are supposedly his fingernails, still growing after his death.

This much we do know: There was a Fodor Glava who was born in Transylvania and died in Lafayette in December 1918. He bought the plot in the middle of the paupers' graveyard. Whether or not he was actually buried there is uncertain. Hundreds of destitute and lonely

Everybody Loves Ramen

If your idea of a burning question is one of the following: (1) What's the perfect wine to pair with ramen noodles?, (2) What is the plural of ramen?, or even (3) Is it possible to make ramen from scratch?, you should waste no time logging onto the Official Ramen Web site (www.mattfischer.com/ramen). Maintained by Fort Collins computer programmer Matt Fischer, this recipe-laden site answers all these important issues and more.

Fischer, who started the Web site when he was a poor, starving college student practically existing on the cheap packages of dry noodles and powdered broth, reckons he gets two or three recipes a day, mostly from college students, though he's noticed a recent upsurge in entries from ex–Wall Street personnel.

At last count, he had 452 ramen-inspired recipes, ranging from ramen fresca (it has feta, roasted garlic, and red onion) to hyperactive choco-ramen (it calls for brown sugar, powdered sugar, chocolate sauce, vanilla, and whipped cream) to mint cookies, a dish Fischer has thus far refused to try. Some places, he says, you just don't want to go. But he has tried recipes using hot dogs, strawberry jam, beer, and, of course, Italian dressing.

He also keeps tabs on recipes for homemade ramen noodles (he claims there is a do-it-yourself contingent of ramen fans) and sporting events involving the ubiquitous blocks of dry noodles and their accompanying flavor packets.

He also knows where ramen originated (Japan, where waits at ramen shops, known as *ramenya*, can last up to three hours), the year instant ramen was developed (1958), and how many packages the average American eats per year (the answer for you Trivial Pursuit junkies is nine).

As for the burning questions we posed in the first paragraph, I can stand the suspense no longer. The answers (according to the noodle guru himself) are (1) Boone's Farm wine; (2) ramen (he's seen the plural as *ramens* but begs to differ); and (3) yes, to make ramen noodles from scratch, combine 2 cups of flour, four eggs, a pinch of salt, 1 tablespoon of water, then roll the dough through a pasta machine with the angel hair attachment.

Need the recipe for Girl Scout Thin Mint Ramen on a stick?
Matt Fischer

★ ★

folks were buried there in 1918, at the height of a deadly influenza epidemic that caused the whole town to be quarantined. His is the only one with an actual marker. As for the writing on the marker, it is shaky and crude as if scratched in haste, but does that mean he was a vampire? We'll let you decide.

The Lafayette Municipal Cemetery is located at 111 West Baseline Road, next to the Bob L. Burger Recreation Center. If you seek further information, call the city clerk's office at (303) 665-5588.

If I Only Had a Heart

Loveland

Sure, you could send your lover a valentine from Poughkeepsie. Or from Sacramento. But why not go all out next Valentine's Day and send your beloved a card postmarked from the city of love?

Yes, Loveland gets a lot of mileage from its romantic-sounding name. The fact that it was actually named after William Loveland, a former general who later became president of Colorado Central Railroad, is beside the point. Remember, it's the thought that counts.

For nearly sixty years, the post office has been adding a message from Cupid (okay, so it's actually a pink cancellation) to all valentines that come its way. It all started in 1947, when Elmer Ives, the postmaster at that time, suggested to the president of the chamber of commerce that they ought to take advantage of their name. The Loveland Valentine Re-Mailing program has been going strong ever since. Last I heard, more than six million notes from Cupid had been sent.

If you want to send your sweetheart a valentine postmarked with an official note from Cupid, send it prestamped and preaddressed in a large first-class envelope to this address: Attn: Postmaster, Valentines, Loveland, CO 80538-9998. But keep in mind it has to arrive in Loveland by February 9.

★ ★

Open Sesame
Loveland

When Connie Kogler spotted a rare streak-backed oriole in her backyard in Loveland, she did something the ubiquitous "they say" would
definitely frown upon. She opened her home to other birders—even
when she wasn't there. For nine days friends and strangers alike, some
that drove from as far away as Winnipeg, Canada, crowded her home
to catch a glimpse of the bright orange-and-red Mexican bird that
rarely, if ever, flies north of the border. She left instructional notes
on the door and kitchen counter and a guest book that eventually
included 413 people who came to see the oriole, nicknamed Pedro
and then later Pedro Maria when Kogler found out it was female.
Visitors from Maryland, Wyoming, Nebraska, New Jersey, Alaska, and
Kansas left suet, oranges, birdseed, cookies, fudge, and cash for her

**Mexican bird makes it through immigra-
tion without a passport.** Connie Kogler

mealworm fund. Pedro Maria, it turns out, was one hungry oriole. She averaged as many as twelve mealworms during her regular morning visits to Kogler's feeder. Alas, on January 1, 2008, she downed 103 mealworms in preparation for her long journey back to Mexico.

Kogler, a mom of three boys and eight girls, had already added 350 birds to her life list when Pedro Maria made her appearance. She has been a bird fanatic since she was eleven. Her cell phone rings bird songs, and her husband, Al, rigged speakers so she can hear outdoor birds inside. Still, trusting more than 400 strangers with the "key" to her home might be considered going overboard. But for her generosity, she was named *WildBird* magazine's 2008 birder of the year and was given a pair of fancy Swarovski binoculars and an all-expenses-paid trip to Costa Rica.

"I really feel that little bird was a gift from God," she says.

Lions and Tigers and Scrap Metal, Oh My!
Timnath

Perhaps the only "zoo" in the world without a monthly vet bill, the Swetsville Zoo in Timnath is a menagerie of, well . . . let's just call them scrap metal animals. The zoo—which is always open and doesn't cost a penny to visit—has dinosaurs made from farm machinery, a swan made from a motorcycle gas tank, a bird made from the rear axle of a pickup, and 170 other animals, all of which have names and a story. The dragon twins, Yin and Yang, for example, guard the entrance to the zoo, and Puff, a two-headed winged dragon, overlooks the Poudre River. The Ali Senior, a 2,000-pound, 20-foot allosaurus, is big enough to hold a picnic under.

The zookeeper is Bill Swet, a retired dairy farmer who has spent the last twenty years building these humorous and whimsical creatures, a pretty impressive feat when you learn he's never had training as a welder, a class in art, or even a hankering to do much of anything but marry his childhood sweetheart, Sandy, and run the family farm.

It all started in 1985, when Swet, a volunteer firefighter, couldn't

Junkyard dinosaur.
Swetsville Zoo

sleep after pulling a man out of a fiery wreck. At 2 a.m., he headed to his shop to try to duplicate a bird ornament he'd admired in a friend's lawn. Using a lathe from 1885 and a 1930s copper welder, Swet constructed a bird with a shovel for a beak and a bike for a body. And for some reason (his most common question is, Is this guy crazy or what?), he just kept right on going, churning out an average of fifteen pieces a year. Luckily, he has two friends with junkyards.

The Swetsville Zoo, which gets 20,000 visitors a year, has three sections: the sculpture park, the Bungled Jungle, and the Museum of Antique Oddities, which includes antique tractors and a bicycle with ten seats.

To take a self-guided tour (just pick up a laminated printed guide at the front gate) of the more than 170 animals with Swet's XS bar brand on their left hips, take I-25 north of Fort Collins to 4801 East Harmony Road. Phone (970) 484-9509.

Someone's in the Freezer with Grandpa

Although he didn't win Jay Leno's "most interesting guy in Colorado" competition (Avvie, an avalanche dog from Breckenridge, captured those honors), Grandpa Bredo Morstoel, who is frozen at −109 degrees Fahrenheit in a vault outside Nederland, was in the running.

In fact, Bo Shaffer, Grandpa Bredo's spokesperson (a necessity since it's rather difficult for a cryogenically preserved talk show guest to provide compelling-enough repartee), was flown by producers out to LA but dumped after Johnny Carson proceeded to die a day or two before the segment was scheduled. Producers decided it was too soon to make "dead guy" jokes.

The town of Nederland certainly gets a lot of mileage out of dead guy jokes. In fact, it stages yearly Frozen Dead Guy Days, complete with a pancake breakfast, frozen T-shirt competitions, hourly tours around the shed where Grandpa is frozen, a Grandpa look-alike contest, and coffin races. There's also a viewing of the film about Bredo, *Grandpa's in the Tuff Shed*.

Born in Norway in 1900, Grandpa Bredo died (at least his heart stopped beating) in 1989, but thanks to the foresight of his grandson, he was cryogenically prepared and frozen in LA, awaiting the day the cure for what killed him is discovered. He currently resides in a Tuff Shed emblazoned with the logo of a Denver radio station. The shed is next to a partially finished, concrete-covered, earthquake-, fire-, and bombproof metal structure that was originally intended to be the main building of the Life Extension Institute, which was started by Bredo's grandson, Trygve Bauge.

Before he could finish, Bauge ran afoul of immigration law, and next thing he knew, he was deported to Norway. As Trygve was leaving, he prevailed on friends to continue keeping Grandpa's body as cold as possible with dry ice. At the time, allowing dead bodies to lie around was pretty controversial in Nederland, so city fathers promptly fixed the loophole by making it illegal. But even city fathers can't make a current situation illegal, so Grandpa Bredo was grandfathered in, so to speak. He's still in Nederland as a resident alien. (He had a roommate, Al, but once his family got wind of the ruckus, they shipped him back to Chicago and stuck him in the ground.)

In 2001 Delta Tech (that's who Bo Shaffer works for, and every four to five weeks he hauls nearly a ton of dry ice up to the shed) and Fox Radio gave Grandpa Bredo a birthday party. He was 101. A slice of cake was added to the crypt to keep him going until the next millennium. Find out more at www.frozendeadguy.com.

Carlye Calvin

3

Denver

In many ways, the entire state of Colorado is a curiosity. If you want to get high (and I'm not talking about the Cheech and Chong kind of high), this is the place to go. Colorado has fifty-four 14-footers, as its 14,000-foot mountains are affectionately called. These are big mountains, folks, mountains that everyday Joes should not attempt at home.

Not that they could. Colorado is the only state to have this many oxygen-requiring hills. Three-fourths of the United States' land that's over 10,000 feet is located in Colorado. Even its lowest point is higher than many states' highest points.

Denver, the state's capital, is, as I'm sure you know, a whole mile above sea level. Step 13 of the capitol building points out this amazing fact, although engineering students from CSU discovered in 1969 that the inscription engraved into the stone step in 1947 (since vandals kept commandeering the sign) was three steps shy of 5,280 feet. They had a geodetic survey plug embedded in the more accurate sixteenth step that very same year.

Another place to get "mile-high" is the row of purple seats in the upper deck at Coors Field, the Rockies baseball team's brick stadium. In fact, Grammy-winning songwriter Randy Newman, a misguided Dodgers fan, commented that if he were named commissioner of baseball, his first move would be to "lower Denver."

Even the man Denver was named for (James William Denver, the governor of territorial Kansas, which, at one time, included parts of

Colorado politicians not only have hot air but also high air.
Denver Metro Convention Bureau

Colorado) was high—or I guess we call that trait "tall" when it occurs in human beings. In fact, the 6-foot-2-inch lawyer who abandoned his promising law practice to lead a troop of tall volunteers (his squadron averaged 6 feet tall, a complete oddity for 1847) into the Mexican-American War would have probably been president of the United States if he hadn't killed a man in a pre–Civil War duel. You know how pesky those political reporters can be.

But enough about politics. This chapter centers on Colorado's capital, its nearby neighbors, and some of its quirky historical characters who may or may not have been affected by the altitude. Denver, which like most of Colorado sprang up because of gold flakes, has the world's largest (and probably most controversial) airport and makes more beer and has more parks than any city in the country.

✦ ✦

Where's the Voom When You Need It?
Above 10,000 Feet

It's an adage every second-grader knows by heart, along with "Don't hit your sister" and "Always wear clean underwear." The adage, of course, is "Don't eat yellow snow."

The problem in Colorado is that in addition to yellow snow and the garden-variety white snow, there's also red snow, commonly known as "watermelon snow." When you first see it, you suspect foul play, wonder who murdered whom.

But rest assured, watermelon snow is not a case for Sherlock Holmes. It's merely a sign that you're high enough in the mountains that a one-celled plant organism called *Chlamydomonas nivalis* is thriving. While this tongue-twisting organism sounds like something to have treated at the local health clinic, it's actually a member of the green algae family that, in addition to chlorophyll, also happens to contain the same carotenoid pigment found in tomatoes, red peppers, autumn leaves, and pink flamingos. It's one of 350 kinds of algae that live in harsh, cold temperatures. The pink pigment, as it turns out, protects the algae from high-altitude ultraviolet radiation.

If you walk through watermelon snow, the soles of your hiking boots will turn pink. And while the Cat in the Hat used Voom, carried in the hat of Little Cat Z, to turn pink snow back to white, there's not a lot you can do with Colorado's pink snow. Except add this little piece of advice to your repertoire: Don't eat yellow *or red* snow. Red snow can cause diarrhea.

To see red snow, visit any of Colorado's fifty-four 14-footers in the spring.

Hot Diggety Dog
Bailey

As you can imagine, the residents of Aspen Park were not exactly overjoyed when Beverly and Jan Slager decided to tote a 14-ton, 42-foot hot dog to their little burg on US 285. After all, the Paul

★ ★

The largest hot dog in the West.
Ron Ruhoff/Coney Island

Bunyan–sized snack stand had already been booted out of Denver, never quite realizing the franchising possibilities Marcus R. Shannon and Lloyd Williams had envisioned when they first patented the unique architectural design on April 12, 1966. By 1969 their hot dog empire dreams had gone up in smoke, but the Slagers were not to be deterred. They bought the monstrosity with its 34-foot bun, hauled it on a huge flatbed truck, and parked on Conifer Road, where it dispensed wieners for more than thirty years.

Eventually, the residents of Aspen Park came to embrace their giant wienie. When Coney Island Hot Dogs went up for sale in 1999, the populace was outraged. A campaign was waged to save the historic landmark. Luckily, a new owner stepped forward with $765,000, the asking price at that time for a 42-foot hot dog, to champion the oversize wiener that locals now know and love. But alas, in late 2005, the landmark frank-in-a-bun faced eviction by developers of a shopping center. When its doors closed on March 5, 2006, the waiting line extended for miles.

The good news is that the concession was purchased and moved—on a flatbed tractor trailer—to Bailey, where it reopened in July 2006.

The giant wienie that operates as Coney Island Hot Dogs is located on US 285 at 10 Old Stagecoach Road. Phone (303) 838-4210.

How's the Mare Up There?

Denver

If you think storing your living room furniture can be a hassle, imagine how artist Donald Lipski felt when he heard the public school in Washington Heights, New York, didn't like the 21-foot-tall sculpture

Don't jump!
Denver Metro Convention Bureau

★ ★

Trivia

Denver's Colfax Avenue is America's longest continuous street, stretching 30 miles through the Mile-High City.

of a red chair they'd commissioned him to make. According to Lipski, the giant chair itself wasn't the problem. The principal objected to the fiberglass pinto pony standing on top.

Originally displayed in Central Park, the two-story steel chair sculpture with the brown-and-white pinto wasn't exactly something Lipski could tuck into the backseat of his car until another buyer came along. Although the Washington Heights Board of Education was willing to trade *The Yearling* for a series of twenty sculptures made from musical instruments, he still had the problem of where to warehouse the gigantic piece of art.

Thankfully, the Denver Art, Culture and Film Foundation stepped up and in 1998 agreed to take the controversial statue off Lipski's hands, greatly decreasing his storage bill. It has been on the lawn of the main Denver Public Library ever since.

The controversial pony that sits between the library and the art museum is located at the corner of Fourteenth and Broadway, catty-corner from the state capitol.

Say Cheese . . . burger!

Denver

I've got some tragic news for the folks of Pasadena, California. You know that cheeseburger you've been calling the world's first? Well, it's not. The first cheeseburger—or at least the first trademark for a cheeseburger—was captured right here in the good state of Colorado. In Denver, in fact, when Louis Ballast, who ran the Humpty Dumpty Barrel Drive-In, filed an official application to trademark the world's first cheeseburger. It was March 5, 1935.

★ ★

Unfortunately, Ballast never became a wealthy man, a fact that didn't seem to bother him. He was too busy plopping new toppings on the basic hamburger that first debuted at the 1904 St. Louis World's Fair. Born in 1910, Ballast was a high school dropout who worked at a furniture store until, at age twenty, he bought the drive-in known around town simply as "The Barrel" because of its shape. Whenever business was slow, Ballast tinkered with the basic burger, adding, among other things, peanut butter and a melted Hershey bar.

While customers quite rightly turned up their noses at those innovations, they seemed to like the burger with the slice of American cheese melted over the top. On March 5, 1935, Ballast headed to the Colorado secretary of state's office to file an application to register the trademark.

Ballast's son, David, still has the trademark application, but his father obviously never attempted to enforce exclusivity to the now-generic name. Nonetheless, the Barrel hung a sign, HOME OF THE ORIGINAL CHEESE-BURGER, which remained unchallenged until the drive-in closed in 1974. And just for the record, the Louis Ballast cheeseburger also had sweet relish, a secret sauce, shredded lettuce, and a toasted bun.

The historic Humpty Dumpty Barrel Drive-In burned to the ground, but there's still a 3-foot granite plaque in the bank parking lot where it once stood. The address is 2776 North Speer Boulevard in Denver.

Curiosities: The Cliff Notes

Denver International Airport

When the city of Denver shuttered Stapleton and moved to DIA, its Office of Art, Culture and Film set aside more than $7 million to decorate the new airport with public art. Lots of the highly lusted-after commissions fell flat on their upturned noses, but the one installation that continues to draw crowds is an oversize map of the United States featuring the very topic of this book: quirky attractions. Artist Gary Sweeney, who doubles as a Continental Airlines baggage handler, not only framed black-and-white photos from childhood family vacations,

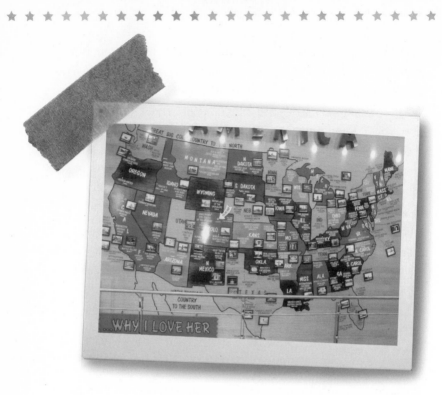

MapQuest for eccentrics.
Carol Keller

but he also used his employee freebies to wage a nationwide curiosities rampage. His gigantic dyed wooden map is dotted with such weird landmarks and offbeat roadside attractions as the world's largest ball of string, the Oyster Museum, and Grandma Prisbey's Bottle Village. Sweeney's installation, a heartfelt adoration of Mother Country, features more than 200 offbeat places and is aptly called *America, Why I Love Her.*

But in one of those ironic twists of fate, at the same time his popular exhibit opened to rave reviews, establishing his national reputation as an artist, his daytime employer closed its Denver hub, and Sweeney got relocated to San Antonio. The good news is he's still making art, still using family snapshots (a recent installation featured him as a kid in a Native American costume with the caption "Long before the abuse and humiliation at Abu Ghraib, there was Cub Scout Pack 849 in Manhattan Beach, California"), and still impressing the public with his sharp wit and *Leave It to Beaver* sensibilities. Among his many unusual creations is a U.S. flag made out of basketballs and parking garage floor signs fashioned from inlaid shoes.

His DIA cluster of marvels is located on opposing walls of the airport near the east baggage claim. Denver International Airport, 8500 Peña Boulevard; (303) 342-2250; www.flydenver.com.

Just Say No!
Denver

Most states would kill to host an Olympics. Heck, Utah practically offered its first-born son to the International Olympics Committee for the right to host the 2002 Olympics in Salt Lake City. Colorado, on the other hand, plays a little harder to get. In fact, when the IOC awarded the 1976 Winter Games to Denver, Colorado became the only state in the history of modern civilization to turn down an Olympic bid.

The IOC awarded the 1976 Winter Olympics to Denver in 1970, but four years before all that glory was to begin, the voters of Colorado turned it down. Keep in mind that winning an Olympic bid is at least as hotly contested as winning a gold medal in figure skating. Or to put it another way, Colorado's "just saying no" was akin to lasting eight episodes on *Survivor* and then looking at the camera and saying, "Just kidding. I don't really want the million dollars."

The landmark vote on November 7, 1972, wasn't even close. A 59.4 percent majority said, "Nope, we don't want to spend our tax dollars on your silly little games." It was a huge reversal from two and a half years earlier, when the Denver delegation came back from the IOC meeting in Amsterdam as conquering heroes. They were greeted with a brass band and a motorcade through downtown Denver for winning the Olympics for Colorado, a diligent effort that began sixteen years earlier when Colorado Springs and Aspen made a joint appeal to get the 1960 Games.

★ ★

But then lawyer Dick Lamm, who two years later won the governorship, started alarming voters with how much an Olympic Games would cost, how detrimental it would be for the environment, and how many heavy-hoofed people would move to their beloved state after witnessing all that Rocky Mountain beauty.

No city, state, or nation had ever rejected the Games before 1972. And it has never happened since.

In retrospect, turning the Olympics away probably wasn't the best idea Colorado ever had. More than thirty years later, it spends beaucoup advertising bucks begging tourists to come ski and camp.

Food, What Food?
Denver

Casa Bonita in west Denver may be the only restaurant in the world where food is beside the point. Not that you leave the 52,000-square-foot restaurant hungry—an all-you-can-eat buffet dishes out the standard Mexican fare. But who has time to eat? Between strolling mariachi bands, Western-style shootouts, puppet shows, a gorilla named Chiquita, flame jugglers, Black Bart's cave, and Mexican dancers, you're lucky to get a taco in edgewise. And if you sit too near the 30-foot waterfall where hunks in trunks dive off cliffs every five minutes or so, your basket of sopapillas is bound to get soggy.

No wonder the creators of South Park devoted a whole episode to Cartman's devious plan to oust Butters from Kyle's birthday party. After all, he was taking his friends to Casa Bonita.

Conceived some thirty years ago by a businessman who got tired of the dry-cleaner business, Casa Bonita and its 85-foot pink stucco tower is the largest restaurant in the Western Hemisphere. It's located at 6715 West Colfax Avenue. Hours are 11 a.m. to 9:30 p.m. Sunday through Thursday, to 10 p.m. Friday and Saturday. For information, call (303) 232-5115, or visit www.casabonitadenver.com.

In the pink.
Bob Von Normann/Casa Bonita

★ ★

Norm, Cliff, and Sitting Bull
Denver

Had *Cheers* been filmed a hundred years earlier, it might have been set at the Buckhorn Exchange, a popular Denver drinking establishment that catered to silver barons, Indian chiefs, gamblers, and roustabouts. Instead of Norm and Cliff, the patrons might have been Sitting Bull and Teddy Roosevelt. And rather than Ted Danson pouring drinks behind the bar, we'd find "Shorty" Zietz, a 4-foot-10-inch former scout of Buffalo Bill's who started the saloon and restaurant in 1893.

Now, that's using your heads.
Buckhorn Exchange

* *

While *Cheers* survived only eleven seasons, the Buckhorn Exchange is alive and well and celebrating its 117th season. As much a museum of the Wild West as a restaurant, this eatery at Tenth and Osage features 517 animal trophies, most of which were shot by Shorty and his son; 120 antique firearms; presidential stationery signed by Teddy Roosevelt; Sitting Bull's grass lariat; and a petrified buffalo chip.

Not only was the Buckhorn awarded Colorado Liquor License Number One, which still hangs behind the bar, but it also has its own ballad and has been on the National Register of Historic Places as long as anybody can remember. The original oak floors and tin roof are still intact; most of the dining room tables, though now covered by red-and-white checkered tablecloths, are converted poker tables; and the murals on the outside wall were painted by local tribesmen who set up their tepees in the Buckhorn parking lot.

Shorty, whose real name was Henry (Sitting Bull, the famous Sioux chief, gave him the nickname), was always a friend to Native Americans. He spoke four native dialects and was known to offer free food to any Indian passing through Denver. When Chief Red Cloud, Sitting Bull's protégé, decided to surrender the military saber he'd snatched from General George Custer in the Battle of the Little Bighorn, he brought it to the Buckhorn along with Sitting Bull's Colt 45.

In the old days, Shorty's biggest clientele worked for the railroad located only yards away. Every Friday, Shorty exchanged the paychecks of railroad employees for gold, a free lunch, and a mug of beer. He also sold saloon tokens that were "legal tender" only at the Buckhorn. Today those tokens are on display, along with a picture of Chief Ironhorse, who modeled for the buffalo nickel; an American flag from Teddy Roosevelt's 1903 train to Colorado (Shorty was his hunting guide); and a two-headed calf that was donated to the Buckhorn after it was found frozen in a field.

Even the Buckhorn's cuisine comes straight from the pages of the Wild West. The house specialty is a combination elk/buffalo plate served with the sauce of the day (cabernet and raisin the day I was

★ ★

Trivia

Among other rare vehicles, Denver's Forney Transportation Museum has Amelia Earhart's "Gold Bug" Kissel, Aly Khan's Rolls Royce, and a trick movie car from Disney's *Herbie Fully Loaded.*

there). The current menu also features alligator, mountain oysters (the Buckhorn sells 2½ tons every year), pheasant, and rattlesnake served with a tantalizing chili and lime sauce.

The Buckhorn's original Dutch lunch added scrapple, a fried mixture of flour and bits of pork, and headcheese, a jellied cheese of hogs' feet, but low demand more or less scrapped that idea. However, T-bone steaks are still a specialty (although the 1½-pound variety that were popular at the beginning of the century have shrunk), as is the ham and bean soup and the homemade Dutch apple pie topped with cinnamon-rum sauce.

The Buckhorn Exchange, at 1000 Osage, is located only five minutes from downtown Denver. It's open seven nights a week for dinner, and lunch is served Monday through Friday. The phone number is (303) 534-9505; www.buckhornexchange.com.

Misdiagnosis
Denver

If it weren't for the Colorado Historical Society and the Denver Medical Society, both organizations that Dr. Frederick Bancroft helped found, his old Denver farmhouse would never have made it onto a mouse pad in the Denver Public Library's Western History Collection, let alone a canvas tote bag. But thanks to his fine contributions to those stellar organizations, the records of history finally forgave him his embarrassing faux pas, namely, his recommendation that Denver gardeners introduce *Taraxacum officinale* into their gardens.

Taraxacum officinale, for those of you who haven't brushed up on your Latin, is a fancy term for dandelion.

In 1920 the pioneer physician, who had a thing for natural English-style gardens, promoted the "tramp with a golden crown," as he called the dandelion, as a method for beautifying the city, providing medicine, and making wine. By 1926, however, it was obvious to everyone that Dr. Bancroft's flower remedy had backfired. *T. officinale* proved to be such an insidious pest that citywide campaigns were waged to "exterminate the dandelion." The *Denver Post* even offered to pay unemployed folks $3 a day to root them up.

Maybe early dandelion planters should have questioned the doctor's orders. After all, Dr. Bancroft, who weighed 250 pounds, was legendary for eating and drinking twice as much red meat and red wine as everyone else and was known to inform patients they were underweight.

To buy a mouse pad or tote bag of Dr. Frederick Bancroft's Denver home, check out the Western History Collection at the Denver Public Library, or find the items for sale at www.cafepress.com/denverlibrary.

Is That a House or a Mushroom?
Golden

It has been called many things: a flying clam, a spaceship, an oversize electric razor. But the modernistic house that's perched on Genesee Mountain is most commonly known as the star of Woody Allen's 1973 movie *Sleeper*. It's also the youngest house ever to win a spot on the National Register of Historic Places.

Designed by Charles Deaton (an architect who said, "People aren't angular, so why should they live in rectangles?"), the famous house with the spectacular views of both Denver to the east and the mountains to the north began life in 1963. It took thirty-seven years to finish the project that Deaton conceived as both a home and a piece of

★ ★

Look, it's a . . . a . . . a . . .
Nick Antonopoulos

art. By 1966 he'd finished the sculptured exterior, which won awards and raves in the press, but unfortunately he didn't have the money to finish the interior. When the *New York Times* ran an article about the architectural wonder that looked like something George Jetson might live in, Woody Allen decided to use it as the home and laboratory of his *Sleeper* protagonist, Miles Monroe, who is defrosted after 200 years of cryogenic sleep.

Filming in Colorado put the neurotic New Yorker to the ultimate test. Not only was there an unpredicted spring blizzard, but a plague of ticks flew into the set. Nonetheless, the house, which is a true Colorado landmark, had a starring role.

In 1991 Deaton finally sold the still-unfinished house to a California businessman for $800,000, but the new owner eventually lost interest, and it sat vacant for several years. When Denver software magnate John Huggins bought it in 1999, all the windows were broken, there was 4 feet of snow in the living room, and a fox had set up residence in one of the five bedrooms. Huggins hired interior decorator Charlee Deaton, Charles's daughter, and her husband, architect Nick Antonopoulos, to complete the first Deaton's dream.

Internationally recognized as one of the finest examples of modern organic architecture, the 7,500-square-foot home has three levels, five bedrooms, five bathrooms, a four-car garage, and a media room. And last I heard, it was for sale again for a mere $10 million.

The *Sleeper* House and its famous Orgasmatron (it's actually a circular tube elevator) is perched on Genesee Mountain, and, while it's not open for tours, you can easily spot it from I-70 at the Genesee exit.

Holy Water
Golden

Back in the Old West, people used to say that "whiskey was for drinkin', and water was for fightin'." The water at the Mother Cabrini Shrine in Golden, however, is used for healing.

Not that the Catholic Church comes right out and says it. All church officials will nod about is that the shrine with the 22-foot statue of Jesus and the 373-step "Stairway of Peace" is an homage to Mother Frances Xavier Cabrini, the first American to be declared a saint. But ask the 150,000 visitors who troop to the shrine each year, and they'll tell you about (no, they'll swear by) the water's healing powers. This holy water has reportedly made blind people see, stomach problems disappear, and dogs live five years longer than predicted. Many come to get the water for friends suffering from diseases or relatives about to undergo surgery.

Mother Cabrini bought the property, which she ran as a summer camp for over 200 immigrant orphans, in 1912. The guy that sold it to her thought he'd pull a fast one on the saint-to-be. After all, the government already declared it as lacking water. And besides, only a fool would set up shop at 7,200 feet above sea level. But shortly

She can't fly, but, boy, does she know how to find water.
Mother Cabrini Shrine

★ ★

after she bought it, Mother Cabrini tapped a rock with her cane, and water gushed from the ground. The spring that's now housed in a small stone building has never stopped, nor has it ever frozen, miracle enough for some folks.

To visit the shrine, which is near the Buffalo Bill Museum & Grave, take I-70 west to Morrison exit 259 or I-70 east to exit 256 and follow the signs. The address is 20189 Cabrini Boulevard; call (303) 526-0758, or visit mothercabrinishrine.org.

The Other World Cup
Highlands Ranch

Pyramids aren't just for cheerleaders anymore. Turns out, there's a new sport, developed in Highlands Ranch, that involves stacking plastic cups in pyramids. The World Sport Stacking Association (WSSA) sanctions tournaments with five events—three for individual cup stackers, one for doubles cup stackers, and a cup-stacking team relay. Developed in 2001 by Bob Fox, a PE teacher, the infant sport (they call it a track meet for your hands) has competitors in sixteen countries. Fox developed the sport, the rules, and the equipment (his company, Speed Stacks, manufactures the heavy plastic cups used in tournaments and metal cups that are used for training) after seeing a Southern California Boys and Girls Club stacking cups on TV. Steven Purugganan, an eleven-year-old from Massachusetts, currently holds three of the speed stacking world records, a feat that was highlighted on ESPN. Every year, the WSSA also hosts what they call a stack-off, with a *Guinness*-listed record of 22,000 cup stackers. Competitors in this riveting sport that, according to Fox, uses both sides of the brain range from ages four to eighty-seven. The WSSA can be reached at P.O. Box 630526, Highlands Ranch, CO 80163; (303) 962-5672; www.worldsportstackingassociation.org.

No Shirt, No Pants, No Problem
Indian Hills

At the Mountain Air Ranch, a 150-acre hideaway southwest of Denver, guests hike, swim, and play horseshoes, volleyball, and bocce ball in nothing but their birthday suits. Twice voted as the most friendly resort in America by the American Association for Nude Recreation (AANR), Mountain Air Ranch was started in 1935 by Alice and John Garrison, only back then it was known as the Colorado Sunshine Club and before that, the Mile-High Health Club. In those days, before people could appreciate the freedom in not being valued for their designer duds, the infamous club frequently changed its name to fool law enforcement officials who didn't take kindly to adults playing dominoes in the buff. On February 19, 1935, the Denver police raided the Garrisons and arrested twenty, including a Methodist Episcopal minister. They were found guilty and fined $1 each.

Today, family-friendly Mountain Air Ranch has 500 members, a women's body support group, and a restaurant aptly called The Lost Bikini Grill.

Mountain Air Ranch, P.O. Box 855, Indian Hills, CO 80454-0855; (303) 697-4083; www.trynude.com.

What's Up, Doc?
Lakewood

I don't understand why Warner Brothers got their knickers in such a snarl. The wabbit on the neon sign outside the Bugs Bunny Motel in Lakewood looks nothing like the famous carrot-chomping cartoon character. I mean, even Elmer Fudd wouldn't have wasted a shot. But in 1997, forty-five years after the nonrelated wabbit was erected on the Colfax Strip, the media giant decided it was necessary to protect itself from the tiny motel in Lakewood. Upon threat of legal action, the owners of the Bugs Bunny Motel wisely decided to change the name.

Now the tall neon rabbit with the carrot and the salt shaker advertises the Big Bunny Motel, but if you look closely at the unlighted

★ ★

tubes behind the blank, you can still see the *U* and the *S*. Locals that have been driving by the familiar landmark for a half century still refer to it as the Bugs Bunny. But let's keep that between ourselves.

According to Richard J. Gardner from Roadside Attractions, the little brick motel has nearly as dramatic a history as its sign. Back when it was still the Bugs Bunny, it played host to actress Sue Lyon, who played the young lead in Stanley Kubrick's film *Lolita*. At the time, eleven years after she won a Golden Globe for her role, she was working as a cocktail waitress and dating Gary Cotton Adamson, who was serving time at the nearby Colorado State Penitentiary. She was evidently having a bad hair day, because she threatened to commit suicide by plunging to her death from one of the motel's windows. The cops, needless to say, thought about responding but then remembered the Bugs Bunny was only one story tall.

The infamous motel is located at 6218 West Colfax Avenue, Lakewood. To make reservations, call (303) 238-6390.

Beer Drinker of the Year
LoDo, Denver

City mayors worldwide are known to give out awards—for citizenship, for best architecture, for best teacher. But Denver's current mayor, John Hickenlooper, gives out an annual award for best beer drinker. Or rather, his company does. And he's the one who came up with the national competition (years ago, before his mayoral run) to focus the spotlight on craft beer making.

Although he sold Wynkoop Brewing, in Lower Downtown Denver, his beer drinker of the year competition is still going strong. Wynkoop puts out a yearly call for beer résumés. The chosen résumé wins its owner the much-coveted title of Beerdrinker of the Year. Not only does the lucky winner get free beer for life at Wynkoop, but also $250 worth of beer at his or her local brewpub. Résumés come in from all over the country. A good beer résumé, according to Wynkoop's official application, includes a complete list (not to exceed

★ ★

three pages) of accomplishments in brewpubs, beer festivals, and beer adventures.

After whittling down the many résumés, Wynkoop flies the top three finalists in to Denver (in ten years, only one Coloradoan has made the finals) for a daylong competition that rivals anything Miss America candidates are asked to do. They weigh in, dispense personal beer philosophy, conduct taste tests, and answer questions about beer. They're also asked to whisper to their beer (hey, it works with horses) and entertain (and sometimes bribe) the judges, who wear robes and white wigs—just like the British magistrates.

If you want to apply for Beerdrinker of the Year (it's a national competition), check out the Wynkoop Brewery Web site at www .wynkoop.com. The brewery itself is located at 1634 18th Street, or you can call them at (303) 297-2700.

Wiggin' out for some brewskis.
Wynkoop Brewing Company

Got Beer?

Colorado as a whole is known as "The Napa Valley of the Beer World." It leads the nation in beer production per capita and has more microbreweries than any other state.

Denver, besides being the capital of this great beer-drinking (hic) state, produces more beer than any other city in the country. In fact, the current mayor of Denver, John Hickenlooper, is a beer connoisseur, having opened Denver's first microbrewery back in 1988 after getting laid off from his job as a geologist.

At last count, there were more than a hundred breweries in Colorado, ranging in size from the largest brewery in the world (Coors in Golden) to tiny small-batch brewpubs in scenic mountain towns (Durango, with a population of about 13,000, for example, has four brewpubs).

Colorado is also home to the country's largest beer festival (the Great American Beer Festival), the Brewers Association (for small craft beer makers and other assorted home brewers), the World Beer Cup (it's considered the Olympics of beer making), and the world's first brewery to be powered by the wind (New Belgium Brewery in Fort Collins).

It's not just beer that Coloradoans pour down their gullets either. With a mild climate and low humidity, Colorado is an ideal place to cultivate grapes that are transformed into sweet, high-altitude wine. The state also claims more than fifty vineyards.

Coors in Golden, Anheuser-Busch and New Belgium in Fort Collins, Rockies Brewing Company in Boulder, Bristol Brewing in Colorado Springs, and other Colorado breweries offer tours. For a complete list of the state's breweries, along with their tours and tastings, visit www.beertown.org.

★ ★

Bison-tennial
Morrison

When President Bill Clinton hosted the world's leaders at the 1997
Summit of Eight, he wasted no time making restaurant reservations
at The Fort in Morrison. He wanted to show Jacques Chirac, Tony
Blair, and other heads of state what eating was like for America's
early pioneers. After discussing the AIDS crisis, third-world debt, and
other blood-curdling topics, the world's bigwigs needed a diversion,
which Fort owner Sam Arnold gladly provided with bison tongue, bull
testicles, gunpowder whiskey, and other unique dishes that he has
developed in forty-five years as a food historian. He also introduced
them to the mountain man toast, which goes like this: "Here's to the
childs what come afore, and here's to the pilgrims what's come arter.
May yer trails be free of grizzlies, your packs filled with plews, and
may you have fat buffler in your pot. WAUGH!"

Not only is Arnold's restaurant an exact replica of Bent's Fort, a
famous fur-trading fort from the 1830s (see entry in Chapter 1), but
it also showcases the culture, the music, and the history of that Wild
West period. When the former ad exec bought the scenic seven-acre
plot with the intention of replicating the old Santa Fe Trail fort with
its 2-foot adobe walls, hand-hewn beams, and earthen and ox blood
floors, the bank turned him down flat. That's when he decided to
build a restaurant instead (the fact that he planned to live on the second floor was beside the point). The Fort's cuisine has always included
buffalo (it's the largest distributor of buffalo steaks in the world), elk,
quail, and other game meats.

The Fort also provides Arnold and his daughter, Holly Arnold Kinney,
who is now co-owner, the perfect forum for developing their other
varied interests. Sam, for example, is a historian and has authored several books on the cuisine of the fur trade period. The Fort periodically
offers Native American flute music (Eric "Many Winds" Herrera is usually there on Friday nights), Spanish and Native American art markets
(through the Arnolds' Tesoro Foundation), and helicopter packages that

★ ★

fly you and a friend from Denver International Airport or the Jefferson County airport to The Fort for a five-course gourmet meal.

The Fort is located at 19192 Highway 8, Morrison; phone (303) 697-4771; www.thefort.com.

Highfalutin entertainment.
The Fort

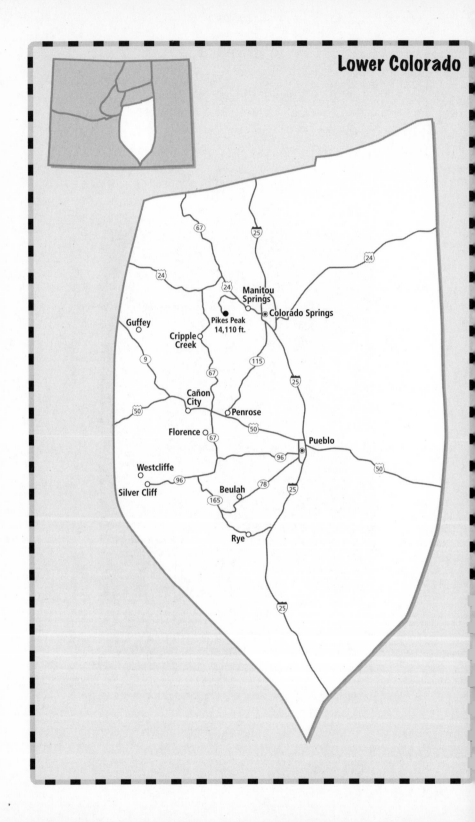

4

Lower Colorado

At an elevation of 6,035 feet, Colorado Springs has two-thirds the oxygen of, say, Miami. Maybe that's why people here push peanuts up Pikes Peak with their nose or celebrate their birthday by climbing the famous mountain again and again, as a mechanical engineer did when he turned thirty-four. He made five trips in twenty-three hours and twenty-nine minutes.

All I know is that within the 100-mile radius of Colorado Springs that's covered in this chapter, people throw fruitcakes, race donkeys, and build gigantic two-story rocking chairs.

Can we blame it on the altitude? I'll let you decide.

★ ★

World's First Rock Star Buried in Colorado

Beulah

In 1876, when Darwin's theory of evolution was first being debated, an entrepreneur named George Hull decided he could make some moola off the heated controversy. Hull made a hush-hush contract with a Colorado artist who agreed to chisel a life-size petrified man with a tail. The 7-foot corpse fashioned from mortar, rock dust, clay, plaster, and ground bones was kiln-fired and buried near Beulah. When it was "accidentally discovered" tangled in the roots of a cedar tree along with a petrified turtle and fish (also made by the artist),

Here lies . . . a huge hoax.
J. Miller Adam

Hull and associate Soapy Smith figured people would line up to see the missing link between man and ape.

They were right. In fact, P. T. Barnum himself at one point offered $20,000 for an interest in the petrified corpse, which became known as the "Solid Muldoon" and went on a profitable national road tour, attracting crowds all the way to New York City. No less an authority than the *Denver Daily Times* said, "There can be no question about the genuineness of this piece of statuary."

Although Darwin never actually laid eyes on the Solid Muldoon, he suspected the petrified corpse was an impostor, and on February 15, 1878, when an associate of Hull's, angry at not getting his fair cut, finally spilled the beans, the Solid Muldoon disappeared. But you can still see his grave, a permanent wooden structure on CO 78 north of Beulah.

Gas Chambers R Us
Cañon City

You might suspect that having the Royal Gorge would be enough tourism for one town. But, oh, how wrong you'd be. Not content to rest on its outdoor wonders, Cañon City also offers tourists the rare chance to see a real-life gas chamber.

At the Museum of Colorado Prisons, tourists can also see the noose used on Colorado's last hanging victim, prison contraband (brass knuckles, tomahawks, and shanks, to name a few), and such disciplinary paraphernalia as cattle prods, whipping racks, balls and chains, and gas guns.

Thirty-two cells are outfitted with exciting exhibits devoted to all aspects of prison life (escape methods, substance abuse, rioting, and, of course, isolation). One cell features an exhibit on eleven-year-old Anton Wood, the youngest person in Colorado ever convicted of murder, and another has an exhibit dedicated to Alferd Packer (see Chapter 2), the only U.S. citizen ever convicted of cannibalism. Still another has a Sheriff Sam robot that relates the career of former warden Roy

★ ★

Best, who wound up in the pokey himself for misuse of public-funded prison lumber. No wonder his bid for governor of Colorado was unsuccessful.

To do time at this unique museum, head to the west side of town, just north of the new prison on First Street and Macon Avenue. (719) 269-3015; www.prisonmuseum.org.

Till death real soon shall we part.
Museum of Colorado Prisons

★ ★

Before Stuntmen
Cañon City

Between 1908 and 1914 the medical profession in Cañon City was
a booming business mainly because Tom Mix and other stars of the
two-reel silent Westerns that were being filmed there insisted on performing their own stunts.

During that time the Selig-Polyscope Motion Picture Company
was located in the Old Reeves Livery Stable, and Cañon City was *the*
place to shoot Westerns. William Selig, the Academy Award–winning
owner of the movie company with the same name, liked the light and
the scenery in Cañon City and, in fact, might still be there except he
heard about this little town out in California called Hollysomething.

So why did Cañon City's doctors profit so handsomely? It was
nothing for Mix and his costars to ride their horses at breakneck
speeds, to plunge into rivers, and to throw violent steers to the
ground. In fact, Mix's fan club claimed that during the filming of
Straight Shooter, he was blown up once, shot at twelve times, and
injured forty-seven times. His arm was in a sling during the entire
filming of *The Bully of Bingo Gulch.*

Though Mix managed to make it out of Cañon City alive when
Selig pulled up stakes and headed to Hollywood, several of Selig's
other employees stuck around town and started the Colorado Film
Company, which continued to make short Westerns in the area until
a starlet named Grace McHugh drowned during filming in 1914.

The Old Reeves Livery Stable, where Selig-Polyscope was located, is
at 224 Main Street.

Where Is the World's Largest Flyswatter When You Need It?
Colorado Springs

I prefer my insects small, thank you very much. But for those who like
big bugs, you can't get much bigger than the 16-foot-tall Hercules
beetle that points the way to the May Natural History Museum of the
Tropics, located (where else?) in Colorado Springs.

★ ★

Finally, a match for Raid!!!
May Natural History Museum

Thank goodness, it's only a replica. The real Hercules beetles, the largest in the world, only get 8 inches long, live in the West Indies, and aren't nearly as fearsome as their 4-inch horns might indicate. Although I've heard that if you accidentally stumble into their flight path, you're risking life and limb.

The gigantic grinning beetle is the perfect mascot for the family-owned museum that also has a Museum of Space Exploration and an RV park. Although the total collection contains more than 100,000 insects, only the top 7,000 or so are on display, including a 17-inch

★ ★

stick insect from New Guinea, a 9-inch scorpion from Africa, and a purple tarantula that's big enough to catch and kill mice.

After eighteen years of trotting around the world showing off his exotic bug collection, John May decided to build a permanent museum on his ranch outside Colorado Springs. As far as I'm concerned, a glass display case is a lot better place to run into half-pound beetles and moths the size of a dinner plate.

The world's largest Hercules beetle is located 9 miles southwest of Colorado Springs, near Fort Carson at 710 Rock Creek Canyon Road. It's open May 1 to October 1. For more information, call the May Museum at (719) 576-0450 or (800) 666-3841; www.maymuseum -camp-rvpark.com/natural_history.htm.

It Appears to Be in the Shape of Bob's Big Boy, Sir
Colorado Springs

The national headquarters of the North American Aerospace Defense Command (NORAD) is located deep inside a mountain at Peterson Air Force Base in Colorado Springs. Manned by a binational military force of Americans and Canadians, the NORAD command keeps a watchful eye on the airspace over North America. Suffice it to say, James Bond would be jealous of all the high-tech gadgets and gizmos.

Built in the early 1960s at the height of the cold war, the fifteen-building mountainside complex required 1½ million tons of dynamite to create the gigantic hole in which it was constructed.

Considered an aging relic until September 11, 2001, NORAD's role in ensuring our national security jumped exponentially after that day. Today, NORAD spends 365 days a year scrutinizing every plane, every ballistic missile, every kite and hang glider with the balls to fly over North American soil. Well, except on Christmas Eve, when NORAD'S high-tech system of radars and satellites turns its attention to the more pressing matter of tracking the big fat guy in the red suit.

NORAD is located at Peterson Air Force Base, adjacent to and east of Colorado Springs off US 24.

★ ★

Coffee, Tea, or Air Tower Nachos
Colorado Springs

These days, it's hard enough to catch a glimpse of an airplane cockpit, let alone sit in one. But at Colorado Springs' aptly named The Airplane Restaurant, a fine dining establishment built around an authentic Boeing KC-97, kids can sit in the pilot's seat, fiddle with the instruments, and pretend to prepare for takeoff.

Steve Kanatzar, a pilot and restaurateur, opened the unique restaurant in May 2002 after scoring one of the country's remaining Boeing KC-97 refueling tankers from the Texas National Air Guard. He shipped it to Colorado from Carswell Air Force Base on eight semitrailers and proceeded to add tables and booths, remote controlled airplanes, autographed photos of plane crews and astronauts, and other memorabilia from one hundred years of aviation history. Guests can spot models of the Red Baron's biplane, jet fighters, and a B-17 that hang from the ceiling. The menu even offers such aviation trivia questions as Name that pilot. The converted fuselage seats 42 diners (another 230 can sit in the main dining room that's perched strategically under the plane's wing, engine, propellers, and all), who are served by a waitstaff decked out in pilots' uniforms. The nearby airport tower frequency is piped over the P.A. system, and the menu features such specialties as air tower nachos, flying fortress fajitas, and, of course, inflight beverages and other jet fuel.

The Airplane Restaurant is located at 1665 North Newport Road; call (719) 570-7656, or visit www.solosrestaurant.com. (Solo's is the former name of the restaurant; the Web address may change in the future.)

Second Amendment Paradise
Colorado Springs

Note to Merrill Lynch: Think automatic weapons. While technology, energy, and dairy stocks plummet, machine guns and other military weaponry are as bullish as ever. Just ask Mel Bernstein, who says the dozens of machine guns he owns continue to be an excellent investment.

"Give you an idea. Twenty-five years ago, this M-16 was $1,500. The cheapest one we've got today is $9,500," he says about his collection of military weaponry that also includes jeeps, tanks, bombs, tents, sleeping bags, medals, boots, boot polish, and serial number belt buckles worn by Hitler's personal SS guards.

His 30,000-square-foot Dragon Arms Military Museum (Mel's nickname is Dragon Man, a moniker he acquired forty years ago after turning a 1967 Harley-Davidson into a dragon that breathes fire) has more than one hundred war vehicles, 1,400 uniforms, hundreds of military weapons, and thousands of artifacts from every American war since World War I, all of which are in pristine working condition. He even built a couple sandbag bunkers filled with mannequins dressed in authentic military garb, using authentic military weapons, even smoking authentic military cigarettes.

"They're even wearing military-issue underwear," Dragon Man pronounces proudly.

Anyone lucky enough to visit swears the Smithsonian's military collections are but a feeble second.

The $3 million collection, registered as a nonprofit, is just one of the businesses Dragon Man, a transplanted New Yorker, runs on his 220-acre compound outside Colorado Springs. He also has a paintball park, a dirt bike track, three shooting ranges (one a labyrinthine pit called Baghdad Village, where Fort Carson soldiers train for specialized combat), and Dragon Man's main business, a motorcycle machine shop.

Once a year, usually in September, Dragon Man and his practical, mild-mannered wife, Terry, host a Machine Gun Invitational where licensed gun enthusiasts from around the country come to fire off machine guns, AK-47s, Uzis, tripod-mounted Gatling guns, and other expensive weaponry. In 2005 the event happened to fall on September 11, so Dragon Man rigged up an effigy of Osama bin Laden between three dynamite and gasoline-loaded automobiles that exploded in a ball of fire when the thousand or so takers began firing off a hundred thousand bullets in Dragon Man's self-created apoca- lyptic war zone.

Dragon Man and Terry give guided tours of their private museum to anyone with $8 and the good sense (at last count, they had seven German shepherds, not to mention all that weaponry) to call ahead. The address is 1200 Dragon Man Drive; call (719) 683-2200, or visit www.dragonmans.com.

Ass You Like It
Cripple Creek

You know how bears used to be a problem at Yellowstone? Tourists fed them and posed with them for photo ops. Well, in Cripple Creek, tourists stay away from the bears, but they sure do feed and pose with the donkeys, wild donkeys that roam the lanes of town like a Los Angeles street gang. So far, other than an occasional overzealous donkey who refuses to vacate the back of an SUV, there haven't been any problems.

In fact, the local Two-Mile-High Club throws yearly fund-raisers to pay the wild donkeys' vet bills and provide extra feed, in case they don't get enough by sticking their heads in the open windows of delighted tourists' cars. Of course, they're also partial to munching on locals' lawns, flower beds, and trash cans.

The wild donkeys, according to the tourist board, are the descen- dants of the donkeys who worked the mines back in the 1890 gold rush. Some of them went blind from never getting out of the mines. Teddy Roosevelt, in fact, who visited Cripple Creek several times dur- ing his presidency, proposed a city ordinance requiring the donkeys be exposed to sunlight at least one hour a day.

Of course, now the donkeys are veritable celebrities, having their own festival at the end of each June. Donkey Derby Days features

Wouldn't squirrels have been easier?
Cripple Creek Welcome Center

amateur donkey races, professional donkey races, and a big human/ donkey race all the way from Victor, Colorado, to Cripple Creek. Donkey Derby Days was started in 1931 by Charley Lehaw, who concluded that since there was a "derby" for every other kind of animal, they might as well have one for the donkeys that came to feed each day at the Palace Drug Store. Charley and a couple other guys built a racetrack, solicited advertising, arranged concessions, and started what is today a successful three-day festival.

For more information about Cripple Creek and its long-standing Donkey Derby Days, call (877) 858-GOLD; www.visitcripplecreek.com/ DonkeyDerbyDays.

★ ★

Rooster Club
Cripple Creek

To be the oldest bar in Cripple Creek, an 1890s mining town that was built on the side of a mountain so as not to disturb the cattle, is no small feat. But what makes the Red Rooster Bar, a small, quiet bar off the lobby of the Imperial Casino Hotel, even more amazing is its collection of 150-plus roosters. Nobody's saying it's the world's largest collection; rather, I would like to suggest it's the world's *onliest* collection of roosters.

Over the years, bar patrons, visiting from around the globe, picked up roosters and sent them back to the cozy bar. Among the cockadoodlers is a nude rooster (I know, what other kind are there?)

Instead of getting up with the chickens, you "get down" with the roosters at Imperial Casino's Red Rooster Bar.
Imperial Casino Hotel

lounging on a settee, a rooster decorating an Italian plate, a rubber rooster, and a stuffed rooster named T. J. Flournoy after the sheriff who turned a blind eye to the Chicken Ranch in La Grange, Texas, for so many years. According to one rumor, T. J., the mascot for the well-known whorehouse, was given to the bar after it was finally shut down in the 1970s.

According to owner Vanessa Hays, who probably has her facts straight, a group of Texans who frequented Cripple Creek's Imperial Hotel made it their mission to present the Red Rooster Bar with a stuffed rooster from the famous ranch that inspired the Broadway musical and later movie *The Best Little Whorehouse in Texas.* One of them volunteered to swipe a rooster and have it stuffed. It has been in the Red Rooster Bar ever since.

The Red Rooster Bar is located at 123 North Third Street in Cripple Creek; phone (800) 235-2922; www.imperialcasinohotel.com.

America's Most Wanted
Florence

If you want bomb-making lessons, you could do worse than showing up in Florence, a tiny Colorado town that just happens to have the highest maximum security prison in the country. At "Supermax," as the federal prison is nicknamed, you could get bomb-making tips from Theodore Kaczynski (the Unabomber), Richard Reid (the shoe bomber), Terry Nichols (the Oklahoma City bomber), and countless other criminals who have mastered the art of nonmilitary bomb making. ADX (Administrative Maximum Facility) Florence specializes in terrorists and serial killers and was also home to Charles Harrelson, actor Woody Harrelson's mobster dad, until he died in March 2007.

You might have trouble getting an appointment, though. All the prisoners are confined to tiny soundproof cells twenty-two to twenty-three hours of every day. Thanks to two solid steel doors, lasers, and silent attack dogs, they're not so much as allowed to talk to one another, let alone prison guards or bomb-making wannabes. When

★ ★

they're not in a cell, they're cuffed, shackled, and escorted by at least two, sometimes three, guards.

The good news is that despite having the most notorious criminals in American history as their next-door neighbors, the people of Florence sleep well knowing that no inmate has ever escaped from this thirty-seven-acre prison that's built into the side of a mountain.

ADX Florence is located on CO 67, 90 miles south of Denver, 45 miles south of Colorado Springs, and 40 miles west of Pueblo. The exact address is 5880 Highway 67, Florence.

Colonel Sanders Theme Park
Guffey

Long before the first Roman candle brightens the night sky, the little town of Guffey celebrates our nation's birthday with a rather unusual flying object. A chicken. Or rather, lots of chickens that are shot out of a fur-lined mailbox mounted on a 12-foot tower. Participants (and if you don't BYOC, you can rent one for $5) pay for the opportunity to place their fine feathered friend in a sky-high mailbox, push it out with a toilet plunger, and see how far it will fly.

Bill Soux, the guy who came up with the annual Fourth of July fund-raiser, was a little worried at first that his scheme might backfire after the first chicken, his, flew a grand total of minus 6 inches. Thankfully, other entrants, while not quite soaring with the eagles, did place better. In fact, the record, set in 2001, stands at 138 feet. No one knows whether Clara Pizzuto, the chicken's trainer who has since retired and moved to Florida, cheated by reading the Trevor Weekes' classic *Teach Your Chicken to Fly Training Manual.* Described on Amazon as "the definitive guide for training inferior fowl to fly," it features detailed diagrams, instructions for building up wing strength, and a thorough list of flying fowl training academies.

Hundreds show up for the event, started in 1986, that also features chicken bingo (like cow bingo, a prize goes to the buyer of the first square to, let's just say, acquire chicken droppings) and a chicken

★ ★

Air mail.
W. A. Soux

rollin' alley, held on an antique bowling alley with pins painted yellow to resemble a chicken.

One year, an animal welfare group called United Poultry Concerns staged a protest, claiming the flyover could cause hens to suffer nervous breakdowns, but they didn't get very far. The mayor of Guffey, a black cat named Monster, wasn't terribly sympathetic. Monster, Guffey's mayor of eight years, won the election in 2001 over Lars, a black lab mix, a pomeranian, and an unhatched cockatiel egg.

If you're interested in participating in the July 4 Chicken Fly, Bill and his wife, Colleen, run a B (that's a B&B without the last *B,* the breakfast). In fact, their rooms, all of which lack running water, range from a converted hog barn to the bunkhouse of an old miner. As for the lack of indoor plumbing, not a problem. Bill and Colleen cheerfully provide each B with their own personal outhouse.

"I have the largest collection of outhouses in Colorado," Bill claims—twenty-eight that are lined up on what Guffey calls "Toilet

Row." You'll know you've arrived when you see the antique prison car with a stuffed dummy in black and white being pulled by a couple of horse skeletons.

Guffey is right off CO 9, exit 21. Bill and Colleen can be reached at P.O. Box 2, Guffey, CO 80820; (719) 689-3291; www.guffeycolorado .com.

Air Fruitcake
Manitou Springs

Whatever you do, don't park on the east side of Memorial Park the first Saturday following New Year's Day, unless, of course, you happen to have flying fruitcake insurance. That's the day of the Great Fruitcake Toss, an annual festival that celebrates the world's most reviled and underappreciated food. Well, celebrating it might be a stretch. The good folks of Manitou Springs fling it, smash it, shoot it with air-powered potato guns, and fashion it into unique sculptures, such as the Saddam Hussein fruitcake bust that landed Dee Byvoet on top of 2005's entrants in the ugliest fruitcake competition. Not to be outdone, her son, Stephen, brought home his own fruitcake trophy—the launch prize—by sending the holiday concoction 285 feet via bow and arrow. Of course, that record has long since been broken by a team of Boeing GPS engineers who flew their fruitcake 1,425½ feet in 2006 when the competition was temporarily held at the high school track, an experiment by the chamber of commerce officials who got tired of cleaning fruitcake off the roofs of area businesses.

Started in 1996, the zany event was moved back to its original location after the chamber came up with a new venue for achieving fruitcake notoriety—catching it in a net. Other categories are tossing (by hand), launching (by catapult), hurling (by any other method), and a Fruitcake Derby that features fruitcakes on wheels. The chamber of commerce provides the ramp. There's still a farthest-traveled competition (recent entries have come from Kuwait and Australia, but I'm sorry to report the Glamour Competition, which has seen such beauts

Fruitcake covergirl.
Manitou Chamber of Commerce

as fruitcakes doubling as stoplights, Pikes Peak, Chia Pets, and baby bottles, has been canceled due to the lack of recent entries.

Although serious entrants BYOF (bring your own fruitcake), area B&Bs have been known to throw in a fruitcake with each room booked, and the event's organizers rent fruitcake for 50 cents apiece.

Not to crash your dreams of glory, but the competition can get pretty fierce. Those Boeing engineers, the ones that hold the current record, built an Omega 380 Fruitcake System from plastic tubing, a compressor, and a stationary bike after getting beat one year by a troop of Girl Scouts. Air Force Major Greg Hillebrand put off driving to D.C. for his new assignment so he could enter his carefully engineered fruitcake catapult. "The movers took everything," he said, "except two sleeping bags and the catapult."

★ ★

The Great Fruitcake Toss is held at Memorial Park (500 block of Manitou Avenue) in Manitou Springs. For more information, contact the Manitou Springs Chamber of Commerce and Visitors Bureau at (719) 685-5089 or (800) 642-2567; www.manitousprings.org.

Rock and Roll
Penrose

The world's largest rocking chair that was featured in the first edition of this book has fallen on hard times. At that time, the 21-foot tall

Just shy of 5 tons, this rocking chair is still the world's heaviest.
Tom and Carol Doxey

rocker was being edged out by a couple wannabes—one in Lipan, Texas, which was taller but weighed less, and one in Hattiesburg, Mississippi, which we didn't think counted because of an embarrassing lack of rockers.

Well, not only did Deadwood, South Dakota, unveil a rocking chair that's 13 feet taller, but the owner of Doxey's Apple Shed Mercantile and Cafe who also owns the Colorado rocker retired so he could travel.

Tom Doxey has gotten lots of offers for the rocker, an impressive piece of carpentry that's made from hand-hewn Douglas fir logs and measures in at 14 feet across, but he refuses to part with it. It stays with the business that's currently up for sale. Although it's behind a barbed wire fence, the former world's largest rocker is located on CO 115, about a mile north of the US 50 intersection. Just shy of 5 tons, this rocking chair is still the world's heaviest.

We're Number Thirty-one

Pikes Peak

Pet rocks, *Desperate Housewives,* and Pikes Peak are living proof that you can sell anything with the right ad campaign. Pikes Peak, which is the most visited mountain on the entire North American continent (it's second in the world behind Japan's Mount Fuji), doesn't even rank in Colorado's top 30 in elevation.

I'm not suggesting Pikes Peak is not spectacular. Why else would Katharine Lee Bates, the Massachusetts English professor, feel inspired to write "America, the Beautiful" after seeing the view from the top? It certainly wasn't for the money. She was paid all of $5 for her efforts.

Still, if you're going to be the symbol of the 1859 gold rush (remember the slogan "Pikes Peak or Bust"?), attract more than a half million people to your summit each year, and be the location of so many famous events (the second-oldest car race, a famous marathon, and a New Year's Eve fireworks show, to name just a few), you'd think you'd at least be required to be in the top 10. Rather, Pikes Peak is the thirty-first tallest of Colorado's mountains.

Last I checked, there were four ways to get to the 14,110-foot summit of Pikes Peak. You can drive the 19-mile Pikes Peak Highway that has a grand total of 156 turns. You can take the Pikes Peak Cog Railway, the highest train in the United States. You can hike Barr's Trail, the 13-mile trail from Manitou Springs. Even though Zebulon Pike, the explorer for whom the famous mountain is named, wrote in his journal that the mountain was "unclimbable," thousands of people do it every year.

The last method for getting to the top of Pikes Peak is to roll a peanut up with your nose, a feat accomplished by Bill Williams in 1929. But don't try that unless you have lots of time. It took him twenty days.

Maybe, instead of wondering why the thirty-first tallest mountain is the most popular, we should just be glad it's still there. In 1938 Colorado governor Teller Ammons lost the state's easternmost peak in a football bet to the governor of Texas. Thank our lucky stars, he won Pikes Peak back before the Texans had it moved south.

Tie One On
Pueblo

Ya know those aprons that Bree Van de Camp of *Desperate Housewives* looks so old-fashioned in? Well, some of them come from Pueblo from a collection owned by Ellyn Anne Geisel, who took up apron gathering after her vacation to a Las Vegas trick riding camp ended up with her getting bit by a horse named Spud. Geisel's collection of 400 aprons morphed into a book (*The Apron Book: Making, Wearing and Sharing a Bit of Cloth and Comfort*), a Smithsonian affiliate traveling exhibit (*Apron Chronicles: A Patchwork of American Recollections*), and her own company (Apron Memories) that sells vintage-inspired aprons.

She got immersed in what she jokingly calls "domestic armor" in

★ ★

1999 after reading obituaries of housewives whose seeming lackluster lives deserved what she calls "a more evocative story." She also created Tie One On Day, where a homemade loaf of bread is tucked in an apron with an encouraging note and taken to a deserving soul. Her apron creations have been featured in *Vogue,* the *Wall Street Journal,* and *Country Living.* Apron Memories, 605 West 17th Street, Pueblo; (877) 9-APRONS; www.apronmemories.com.

Turning Lemons into Lemonade
Pueblo

On June 3, 1921, the Arkansas River flooded the town of Pueblo and claimed 132 of its citizens. To avoid a repeat performance, the city built a levee soon thereafter. While the concrete ditch certainly performed its job, it didn't offer much in the way of aesthetic appeal. Behind its back, the locals even had the nerve to dub its gray walls the "Black Hole of Pueblo," an apt moniker since besides preventing floods, it also carried refuse from the city's steel mills to unsuspecting towns downstream.

A makeover was clearly needed. In the 1970s some college students, late at night with nothing to do, took paint to the 45-degree levee walls. One painting led to two, and before long, city officials decided to make it official, starting what is now known as the Pueblo Levee Project. In an ingenious move normally not attributed to politicians, they decided that rather than dispose of the paint collected during the annual Toxic Waste Day, they'd use the half-filled cans to spruce up the levee. Locals were invited to express themselves however they saw fit. Its 2 miles of art shows off everything from Andy Warhol replicas to depictions of women in history.

The *Guinness World Records* folks clearly recognized the city's genius and declared the mural at 176,000 feet the world's longest, a record it still claims, although impostors have unsuccessfully attempted to break it.

For the best viewing, take the steps by the bridge on Corona

You Only Live Twice or Maybe Three or Four Times

The pueblo home where Virginia "Ginni" Tighe was hypnotized and regressed by tractor salesman Morey Bernstein is now a private residence at 1819 Elizabeth Street. Bernstein popularized hypnosis and the idea of past-life regression in his book *The Search for Bridey Murphy*, which he based on his 1952 hypnosis of Tighe—aka Ruth Simmons in the book—in which she recounted a previous life as Bridey Murphy, an Irish woman from Cork supposedly born in 1798. Though her "regression" was later convincingly discredited, Ginni retained some belief in reincarnation until she died in Denver in 1995, possibly for a second—or perhaps third—time.

Avenue. A hike either way should be enough exercise for the day. If you'd like to make your own contribution to the 2-mile, 58-foot-tall mural (at last count, there were still 3 unpainted miles), call Cynthia Ramu at (719) 549-2737.

One Man's Castle
Rye

When Jim Bishop was fifteen, he dropped out of school, bought two and a half acres of land with the $450 he'd saved mowing lawns and throwing newspapers, and set out to prove that the teacher who claimed he would never amount to anything was wrong—dead wrong.

Ten years later, he started building what he originally thought would be a one-room stone cottage for himself and his wife, Phoebe. When friends started commenting that the stone structure looked more like

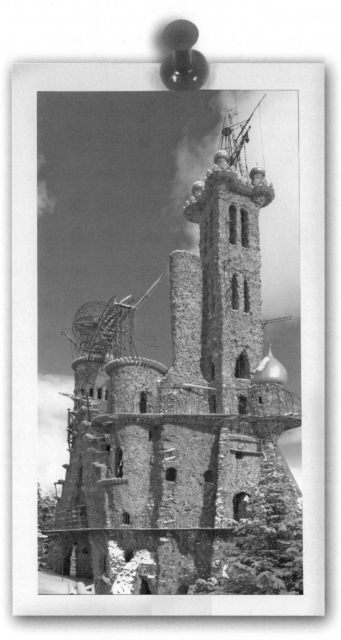

Castles in the air.
J. Miller Adam

★ ★

a castle than a cabin, his imagination was stirred. Before he knew it, Bishop's Castle turned into the world's largest one-man construction project. With his two bare hands, Bishop has hauled and set more than 36 tons of rocks. And he's still at it today, four decades later.

Bishop's ongoing work of art (he says it'll be done the day he doesn't wake up) is now 160 feet tall and has a grand ballroom, stained-glass windows, giant arches, intricate ironwork, and a fire-breathing dragon that's perched 80 feet in the air. It seems that teacher was wrong. Bishop's castle has been featured in *National Geographic* and dozens of other magazines and is visited by thousands each year. If folks show up on a weekend, they'll likely see Bishop himself, bending iron, felling trees, cutting rock, and laying mortar. This is a testament to what one man can do who has no plans, no blueprints, not even drawings, except the ones Jim did to illustrate his opus, *Castle Building from My Point of View*.

Although friends urged Bishop to start charging admission to the hordes of tourists who trekked up the pass to the castle smack dab in the middle of San Isabel National Forest, he refused, insisting that he always hated when he was a kid and couldn't go to the zoo or the ballpark because admission for the whole family was too high. The price of admission will always be free. It's even written into the castle's legal constitution. That's not to say you can't stick a buck or two in the donation box or load up on souvenirs at Phoebe's Castle Keepsakes, which offers, among other things, Jim's book, T-shirts with sketches of the castle, and postcards of the fire-breathing dragon that Jim made from stainless steel warming plates from Pueblo County Hospital and a hot-air balloon burner.

Future plans include a moat and drawbridge, a waterfall, a roller coaster mounted on the outer wall, and a balcony big enough to hold an orchestra.

To visit what Bishop calls "the poor man's Disneyland," take exit 74 off I-25 to CO 165, and drive for approximately 24 miles. Look for the signs. The phone number is (719) 564-4366.

* *

There's No Place like Dome
Silver Cliff

In 1880, two years after a greasy-looking rock from a nearby cliff melted into 75 percent silver, Silver Cliff was the third-largest metropolis in Colorado, lagging only behind Denver and Leadville. Unfortunately, by 1882 the silver boom came to a screeching halt, and most of the fickle businesses and homeowners mounted their buildings onto rollers and scooted them 3 miles over to Westcliffe. The most recent population count put Silver Cliff at 541. A few structures from the heyday remain. There's an old school, a fire station, and the original town hall.

There's also a structure that hasn't been there that long, or if it has, the U.S. Patent and Trademark Office will need to renege on the patent it gave Buckminster Fuller in 1954. The geodesic dome that sits in the middle of Main Street, while it looks like a giant golf ball, is actually a saloon and music hall that has been in business for twenty-five years. In fact, Mary Behrendt says the Silverdome has been open 9,160 consecutive days. And she should know. She's the one working the giant beetle-kill pine bar. Her husband, Charlie, a boilermaker before he started erecting monstrous golf balls, built the dome in 1984 to serve as the town's main watering hole.

It has a big stage on one side that features such acts as the DeWayne Brothers. The Silverdome Saloon & Music Hall is located at 110 Main Street; (719) 783-9458.

Cave Man
Marble Mountains, near Westcliffe

It's not exactly the easiest cave to get to, which could explain why La Caverna del Oro (the Cave of Gold) hasn't been turned into the next Carlsbad Caverns. Oh yes, and the fact that anybody who gets within spitting distance is plagued by demons.

The legend of the cave that's a good 13,000 feet above sea level

★ ★

was passed down from generation to generation by Native Americans. When Spanish explorers showed up on the scene in the fifteenth century, monks translated the rumor about the gold, and by 1541 those greedy Spanish monks overlooked the bit about slavery not being the most Christian pursuit and forced the natives to extract gold from the cave. Finally, the Indians wised up and staged an uprising, killing two of the three monks. The third monk, De la Cruz, convinced the tribesmen that he could subdue the "evil spirits," which he must have done by asking them (those awful spirits) to enter him, because after the Indians brought up vast quantities of gold, De la Cruz killed them all, loaded up the gold on pack mules, and fled back to Mexico.

Fast forward to 1869, when Elisha Horn stumbled upon a skeleton clad in Spanish armor with an arrow sticking out its back. Painted on the rocks above the skeleton was a very faint red Maltese cross that marked the entrance to the cave.

In the 1920s a Colorado Mountain Club group led by a forest ranger went back to the cave. A 105-year-old Mexican woman had told the ranger about the gold and said that when she was a child, she remembered seeing miners trooping out with heaps of gold.

Although the spelunkers didn't find any precious rock or the wooden door guarding the horde of gold the Mexican woman told them about, they did find a 200-year-old ladder and a hammer made in the 1600s. They also found ruins of an old fort and many arrowheads. Other items found over the years are a rope, a bucket, a clay jug, a shovel, and a human skeleton chained by the neck to a wall in the cave.

According to some folks, the Maltese cross marks the back entrance to the cave of gold, and the main entrance where all the gold is still hidden remains to be found. Which brings up a good point: Do I really want to tell you how to find it?

All I'll let out is this: La Caverna del Oro is in the Marble Mountains, just over Music Pass to the northeast of the Great Sand Dunes.

5

Mountain Towns

Back in the '60s, when Bob Dylan was warbling peace ballads and campus protesters were being sprayed with tear gas, I was in Ellsworth, Kansas, perfecting the herkie, an inconsequential cheerleading jump.

Oh sure, I made tie-dyed T-shirts in my mom's washing machine, and I knew all the words to the Beatles' "Love Me Do," but, for the most part, I missed the '60s.

Maybe that's why I like Breckenridge, Leadville, and other Colorado mountain towns so much. The townsfolk, while certainly prosperous, tend to be society dropouts who disdain corporate rules, conservative politics, and anybody who can't ski.

Although they've certainly made concessions for comfort (hey, even the hippies eventually turned in their bell bottoms and beads) with four-star hotels and pricey boutiques, the independent, fiercely liberal spirit persists, as you'll see in this chapter.

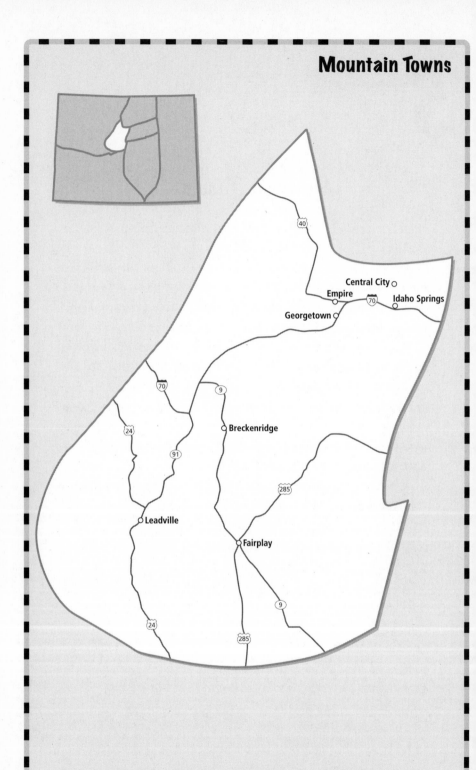

★ ★

Thy Kingdom Come
Breckenridge

When you drive into Breckenridge, you'll notice a rather dubious sign: WELCOME TO THE KINGDOM OF BRECKENRIDGE.

So what gives? Isn't Breckenridge just a regular town? Well, not according to American mapmakers. For a good fifty years, the historic town in Summit County was completely omitted from any and all official Colorado maps. Even though the prosperous town has been around since 1859, when General George Spencer and fourteen prospectors found gold in the Blue River, it somehow got left off all maps and treaties until the mid-1930s. An inept cartographer managed to bypass the entire town, making it a nonentity until the error was finally discovered and righted a half century later.

Hardly the kind of respect you'd expect for a town named after a U.S. vice president—John Breckinridge, the reigning honcho in 1859. It seems General Spencer figured a little sweet talking would help the new 320-acre townsite land a U.S. post office. Although his scheme worked (by the end of the year, 8,000 wannabe miners moved to town, and they indeed got a post office), the indignant natives proceeded to change the town's spelling when the former veep had the gall to join Confederate forces.

To get back at the U.S. mapmakers who neglected them for five decades, Breckenridge used to throw a yearly No Man's Land Festival, where the whole town seceded from the Union, proclaiming itself the independent Kingdom of Breckenridge. In fact, when the 1,500-square-mile section of land that included Breckenridge was officially added to U.S. maps on August 8, 1936, a special proviso was granted: "Breckenridge has the right to be a free and independent kingdom three days each year."

The sign declaring Breckenridge's unique status as a kingdom is located on the left side of the road as you come into town.

★ ★

Is That Gold in That Thar' Blanket?
Breckenridge

Next to the Loch Ness Monster, Bigfoot, and Michael Jackson's nose, one of the world's great mysteries is whatever happened to the 13½-pound gold nugget that Breckenridge miner Tom Groves pulled out of the Blue River on July 23, 1887. True to custom, he had the giant gold nugget verified at the local assayer's office, and he even carried it around town for three days in a blanket, prompting jealous detractors to call the human head–size piece of gold "Tom's baby."

Finally, on July 26, Groves stuck the nugget on a train bound for Denver, hoping to claim his booty. There was just one problem: The gold nugget never turned up. In fact, its whereabouts for eighty-five years are completely unknown. It did finally show up in 1972 when the Colorado State Historical Museum was investigating some old ore specimens deposited in 1926 in a Denver bank. Not only was that too late for Tom to profit from his record-setting find, but his world record had mysteriously lost 5 of its 13½ pounds, qualifying it for a state record surely, but not the world record that it originally held.

The even bigger mystery is where the danged thing was between 1887 and 1926. Unfounded rumors over the years have suggested it was busy being displayed at the Smithsonian, the Peabody Museum, Harvard University, Chicago's Field Museum, and other such stellar institutions, but nobody seems to know for sure.

A replica of Tom's nugget can be viewed at the Breckenridge Town Hall on Ski Hill Road.

Where's the Biff?
Breckenridge

Batman has Bruce Wayne. Superman has Clark Kent. Jeffrey Bergeron has Biff America, the alter ego he uses on his own wacky TV talk show in Breckenridge.

Not only does Biff give zany weather reports (weather, in a ski town, is one of the few things that really matter), he also stages T-shirt fashion shows, reads headlines from the *National Enquirer,* and serves up caffeinated commentary on everything from sex, family, and dead people to avalanche awareness, mountain living, and how to avoid a life of perilous mediocrity. *Backcountry* magazine's publishing arm, Height of the Land Publishing, printed a book containing seventy of Biff's columns. It's called *The Biff America Anthology: Steep, Deep, and Dyslexic,* and as Biff says, "It's a great stocking stuffer for people you hate."

Besides being a well-known radio and TV personality, Biff serves on the Breckenridge Town Council and bikes all across the country. He represents the Green Party (he snagged an interview with Ralph Nader during the 2000 election) and ran on the platform of medicinal marijuana and homeland security. Originally from Massachusetts, Bergeron has lived in Summit County for thirty winters.

"In any other town, I'd be a ski bum," he says. "Here, I'm Biff America."

Biff's show can be seen on RSN cable television, or you can read his columns in the *Summit Daily News.*

Frosty's Days Are Numbered
Breckenridge

When I went to the International Snow Sculpture Championships in Breckenridge, I was expecting glorified snowmen—something like the Snoopy and his doghouse I built in sixth grade. Was I ever surprised, no, awed would be a more appropriate description, to find elaborate two-story sculptures worthy of any art museum. The Chinese entry, for example, was called *Liang Zhu,* and it depicted a Chinese legend where two lovers turned into butterflies after dying for their love.

The Mexican team concocted a sculpture called *The Configuration of Time,* which represented how human relationships change according to the context of space and time. There was also Neptune's throne (sculpted by a team from Morocco); a portrayal of Nanook, the polar bear, hunting for seal; a ghost ship; and a kaleidoscope that you could actually rotate.

Gone with the thawing wind . . .
Carl Scofield

Four-man snow-sculpting teams from around the world start with nothing but a 20-ton block of snow. They use shovels, ice saws, cheese graters, ladders, and even scaffolding to transform the 10-by-20-by-12-foot monster blocks into artistic masterpieces. Each team, using only snow, water, and ice, puts in fifty to sixty-five hours of intense work into the sculptures.

To find out more about the International Snow Sculpture Championships, contact the Resort Chamber at P.O. Box 1909, Breckenridge, CO 80424; call (303) 453-6018, or click on www.gobreck.com. The sculptures can be viewed at Breckenridge's Riverwalk Center.

Parental Guidance Suggested
Breckenridge

Breckenridge's Ullr Parade has been called the world's craziest. I can't vouch for that (crazy, after all, is in the mind of the beholder), but I do know that 20,000 people turning up for any event when temperatures range from −15 to 20 degrees Fahrenheit would indicate something out of the ordinary is going on.

Ullr Fest (it's pronounced OOO-ler, and it helps if you say it with a mouthful of wet spaghetti) pays homage to Ullr, the mythical Norse god of snow. As the story goes, the Norse god got ticked back in the

That's Mr. Sven to you.
Carl Scofield

★ ★

1960s for some reason and forgot to dump his gifts on the ski town. Locals decided to throw a party to woo him back, and Ullr, the son or stepson (it depends on which mythology expert you talk to) of Thor, hasn't let them down since. Locals believe the heartier they party, the more snow they'll get.

The weeklong festival includes the wacky Ullympics (in one event, locals bowl with frozen turkeys, and in another, they ski with 2-by-6-inch planks on their boots), an Ullr Bonfire, and the parade that, according to some folks, is getting a bit R-rated. Streaking, bikinis, and hot tubs are not uncommon. One year the assistant chief of police approached the city council about toning the forty-year tradition down a notch. Turning a blind eye to open-container regulations for an afternoon is one thing, but nudity, especially when more and more families are coming, is another.

I'm happy to report that the town council of Breckenridge said that while they are happy to sanitize lots of things, the Ullr Parade—which has traditionally been fueled by skin, humor, and booze—is not one of them. "The parade and bonfire," quipped one of the council members, "is not necessarily a family event. Of course, a lot of families are created because of it." They did agree to consider a possible disclaimer letting families know that the parade is not for the easily offended.

If you're looking for a place to wear your Viking helmet, check out Ullr Fest (call the Breckenridge Resort Chamber at 970-453-2913 for info). To see a permanent statue of the Norse god, check out the front of the Park Avenue Lofts near the base of Peak 9.

Brew-Ha-Ha
Central City

When Colorado voters passed Amendment 4 in 1991, allowing legalized limited-stakes gambling, Dostal Alley Brewpub and Casino in Central City was the first to jump on the bandwagon—that is, if you can call adding forty-four slots to the cellar of your T-shirt and rock shop jumping on the bandwagon. Now, nearly twenty years later,

Dostal Alley has grown to be . . . well, the smallest casino in America.

Of course, it's tough to expand in a town whose population peaked a century ago at 3,114 and has declined pretty steadily ever since. Tougher still to make room for more slot machines in a building from 1878 that originally was a tiny miners' grocery, especially when you share the space with a brewpub and an Italian restaurant. Dostal Alley has managed to grow to seventy-one slots, but don't expect any blackjack or craps dealers. Dostal Alley Brewpub and Casino is located at 114–116 Main Street, Central City; and can be reached at (303) 582-1610.

Three Faces of Eve

Central City

Along with Pikes Peak, one of Colorado's most popular tourist attractions is a mysterious painting on a barroom floor. Every year, thousands of folks come to the Face Bar Restaurant in the Teller House to gawk at the painting of the beautiful woman and wonder, "Who is she?" and "Why is she there?"

For years, no one had a clue. Tour guides, as tour guides tend to do, made up a story. They claimed it was a painting of the infamous Baby Doe, whose husband, Horace Tabor, took over senatorial duties from Henry Teller, who built the hotel that at one time was the ritziest accommodations in the West. When Ulysses S. Grant visited, local mine owners laid twenty-six ingots of solid silver to make a path to the hotel so he wouldn't have to dirty his boots when stepping from his carriage.

Others said the mysterious face was the Madeline from H. Antoine D'Arcy's poem "The Face Upon the Floor." All we knew for a long time was that it had inspired a country-and-western song and that one of the most popular short operas in American history was written about it. *The Face on the Barroom Floor* by Henry Mollicone was originally written for the Central City Opera Festival before going on to be performed all over the world.

In 1962, when the real painter died, the story of the "face on the barroom floor" was finally revealed. Herndon Davis, a cousin of Confederate president Jefferson Davis, was a sign painter, a mapmaker, and an illustrator for the *Denver Post*. In 1936 he was commissioned to do a series of paintings for the Central City Opera Association and the Teller House. He got in a shouting match over the authenticity of some western art with an influential opera donor. A sixteen-year-old busboy named Joe Libby, who overheard the conversation, challenged the painter with this: "Since you're going to be fired anyway, why not give them something to really remember you by?" After the bar closed that very night, Libby snuck Davis in, poured him a drink, and held a candle as he created the painting that for so many years was a great mystery.

The painting, as it turns out, is not of Baby Doe or of the Madeline from the famous poem, but of Davis's own wife, Nita, who still lived in Denver when Davis died in 1962.

The Teller House is located 120 Eureka Street; call (303) 582-5283.

Between a Rock and a Hard Place
Empire

When the owners of the Hard Rock Cafe chain, the one you probably have at least one T-shirt from, threatened to sue the Hard Rock Cafe in Empire (pop. 355), they were laughed right out of the courtroom. After all, the Hard Rock Cafe in Empire has been around since 1934. The very earliest of the three hundred gazillion (okay, so I'm exaggerating just a little bit) Hard Rock Cafes with all the T-shirts and celebrity owners didn't open until 1971.

In fact, if I were the Empire version, I'd ponder a little lawsuit of my own. Who's to say that when Peter Morton and Isaac Tigrett opened that first glitzy Hard Rock Cafe in London that they hadn't seen the more rustic version in Empire?

Granted, the Empire Hard Rock doesn't have any 20-foot neon guitars outside to advertise the place (in fact, if you don't look closely,

Mick Jagger wasn't even born when this Hard Rock Cafe opened its doors.
Rob Morris

you might miss the small vertical sign outside the small wooden building), but what it does have are lots of great skiers' breakfast specials (like blueberry pancakes), fabulous seven-days-a-week happy hours, and some of the best chicken-fried steak ever spotted north of the Mason-Dixon.

The very first Hard Rock Cafe, which shares office space with the town of Empire (city hall, or what there is of it, is housed upstairs) is located at 18 East Park Avenue. The phone number is (303) 569-2618.

One Season Is Not Enough

Intrepid skiers in Colorado pride themselves on skiing at least once every month. For those diehards, there's St. Mary's Glacier, the southernmost glacier in North America. Like glaciers everywhere, it's shrinking, but St. Mary's offers year-round skiing, snowboarding, and sledding. Of course, you have to hike a steep ¾ mile to get to this Ice Age playground, but with year-round snow, sweeping views of the Continental Divide, and only occasional avalanches, it's worth carrying skis. The "trailhead" for St. Mary's Glacier is 10 miles off I-70 at the St. Mary's/Alice exit.

His Ass Is Grass . . . and Rock-and-Glass-Encased Memorial
Fairplay

The largest gravestone in Fairplay doesn't belong to a mayor or a former astronaut or anybody else you've probably heard of. The most celebrated grave site in all of central Colorado belongs to Prunes, a faithful, shaggy burro who packed supplies to and from every mine in the Fairplay–Alma area. By the time he died in 1930 at the ripe old age of sixty-three, Prunes was missing his teeth, loved by all the miners who tried to nurse him back to health with flapjacks, and worth the two weeks his owner, Rupe Sherwood, spent erecting a 5½-foot stone monument in the center of town.

While Rupe himself was later buried next to Prunes, it's the burro's memorial that gets all the notoriety. There's a poem dedicated to Prunes (it's engraved on the memorial along with the glass-enclosed displays of his harness and shoes), at least one book written about him (the one I've seen is *Two Burros of Fairplay,* which also tells the story of Shorty, another burro who has a fancy gravestone in Fairplay), a geocaching site dedicated to him, and a long-standing burro race in his honor. Called the World Championship Pack Burro Race and billed as the planet's "highest, longest, roughest, and toughest" race, it begins and ends at his memorial, but not before burros and their "owners" carrying pickaxes and prospector's pans reach the summit of Mosquito Pass and back. And, of course, we can't forget Burro Days, Fairplay's Brown Burro Cafe, and a local music festival called Burropalooza.

To see the grave site of the faithful burro who came down from the mines alone with only a shopping list tied to his harness, visit the Hand Hotel at 531 Front Street, one of several dozen historic buildings in Fairplay.

Scared Crooked

The state of Colorado has so many out-of-the-ordinary outhouses that historian Kenneth Jessen managed to write a whole book about them. It's called *Out the Back, Down the Path* and includes 260 pictures. Coloradan Bill Soux goes so far as to collect outhouses (twenty-eight at last count, see Chapter 4) because "they make great toolsheds." He has one that houses nails and screws, another for insulation, yet another for tar paper.

But perhaps the Colorado outhouse with the most notorious and historical connections is Fairplay's very own Leaning Tower of Pea-Zah, an ancient outhouse that, we think, used to be straight.

★ ★

Loo Skywalker
Georgetown

I don't get it. Historic Georgetown, a nonprofit whose sole purpose is preserving the heritage of Georgetown and Silver Plume, doesn't mention the Hamill House outhouse even once on its fancy Web site.

Oh, they point out the Hamill House, all right. In fact, the 1867 Victorian mansion built by Englishman William Hamill, a successful silver mine owner, banker, and politician, is the foundation's pride and joy. It's just that the Web site likes to go on about the lavish house's early Gothic architecture, its antique furnishings, and its gold-plated doorknobs. Those are all interesting features, no doubt, but there must be 9,000 restored Victorian homes in Colorado alone.

But answer me this: How many old Victorian homes can you name that have six-seater outhouses? Yep, the outhouse behind the house that Mark Hamill's (yes, that Mark Hamill) great-great-grandfather built is easily the most ornate in the world. In fact, the outhouse was *so* ornate that the servants were forced to use their own, more humble outhouse next door. But they got back at their employers: They threw their used liquor bottles down the six black walnut holes.

The one-of-a-kind outhouse is located behind the Hamill House at 305 Argentine Street; call (303) 569-2840.

Comic Bas Relief
Idaho Springs

Washington, D.C., has a statue of Abraham Lincoln. Boston has one of John F. Kennedy. Idaho Springs welcomes visitors to its downtown with a statue of Steve Canyon, a Sunday comic strip character.

In fact, in 1947, when patriotism was at an all-time high, the residents of this burg off I-70 renamed their town Steve Canyon as a tribute to the fictional pilot who appeared every Sunday in the funny pages. They even gave Milton Caniff, the cartoonist who created the World War II hero, his own personal gold mine and convinced the federal government to pony up the $12,000 it took to purchase the larger-than-life limestone statue from the Indiana Limestone Company. Formally dedicated on July 8, 1950, the statue has a plaque that reads, "The United States Treasury salutes Steve Canyon and through him, all American cartoon characters who serve the Nation."

The comic book statue is located off I-70 at the Idaho Springs exit. It's right there at the entrance to downtown at Miner Street and Colorado Boulevard.

"Oh My God" Road

A 9-mile dirt-and-gravel stretch between Central City and Idaho Springs is known as the "Oh My God" road. There's even a green highway sign that identifies this treacherous, washboard road as the roller coaster that it is. Originally built for miners back in the 1870s, the "Oh My God" road has nary a guardrail, washed-out shoulders, a 7 percent grade, and a grand total of forty-six switchbacks. Anyone who tries driving it faster than 15 miles an hour should definitely consult the nearest funny farm.

The only reason travelers would ever subject themselves to such a drive is the breathtaking views of Mount Evans and the roadside ghost towns complete with dilapidated miners' cabins, mine shafts, and rusted-out water chutes—oh yeah, and the rumor that chunks of gold are still strewn along Clear Creek. Of course, nobody has a prayer of seeing the gold chunks. They're way too busy clutching the steering wheel, repeating the road's moniker, "Oh my god. Oh my god," or, if they're a passenger, singing, "Please, would ya *please* slow down."

The "Oh My God" road, which on some maps is shown as Virginia Canyon Road, is located between Idaho Springs and Central City.

Move Over, Michelangelo: Colorado's Own Sistine Chapel
Leadville

In 1926 the Reverend George Trunk, a Slovenian priest who spoke six languages, decided his little church in Leadville needed some sprucing up.

Even though he was sixty-two, had absolutely no art training, and could only come up with $79 for paint, he went to work painting every wall, every ceiling, and every bare nook and cranny of his little brick St. Joseph's Church. It took him two years to complete the project consisting of scenes from the Old and New Testaments. And like Michelangelo, he lay for hours on a high scaffold, painting away.

His $79 project, which was finally completed in 1928, is considered to be the finest example of Slovenian folk art in America.

St. Joseph's Catholic Church is located at Second and Maple Streets in Leadville. The phone number is (719) 486-1382.

Ice, Ice Baby
Leadville

If you go to Leadville, you'll probably see the Ice Palace Inn B&B. And it's a nice B&B. The owners are friendly, the rooms are nicely decorated, and the breakfasts are hearty. But there's no way the current Ice Palace can even begin to compare to the short-lived Leadville Ice Palace of 1896. I say 1896 because that's all it lasted. And only three months of 1896 at that. Unseasonable chinook winds melted the spectacular five-acre palace made entirely of ice just eighty-seven days after it was completed. Suffice it to say, that was not enough time to complete its investors' mission—to rescue the flagging mining economy.

The spectacular palace that shimmered like diamonds in the mountain light did attract a quarter million sightseers, but with all the construction overruns (they ran out of ice and had to ship it in from 150 miles away), the prize money (there were all kinds of contests, including best paper dress and best Grover Cleveland imitation), and those untimely chinook winds, the economy didn't get rescued, and the investors lost their shirts.

Not only was the Leadville Ice Palace the largest ice structure ever built, but it also had a ballroom, a theater, a skating rink the size of two football fields (180 feet), a restaurant, a dance floor, and indoor toboggan runs. American Beauty roses and 18-inch trout were frozen in blocks of clear ice to decorate the walls. The palace with the nine-story octagonal towers and the two-story *Lady Leadville* sculpture was built in two months with 5,000 tons of ice and a crew of 250 men who worked around the clock.

But alas, by May 28 it was condemned, and Tingley S. Wood, who raised the money, said if he had his way, he'd blow the Ice Palace off the face of Capitol Hill.

There was talk of rebuilding the ice palace, albeit a smaller version, in 1996, but it never came to pass. Nowadays, the only reminders are the Ice Palace Inn B&B at 813 Spruce Street (800-754-2840; www.ice palaceinn.com) and the miniature replica at the Heritage Museum, 102 East Ninth Street (719-486-1878). Or if you're there in the winter, you can still take the Ice Palace Toboggan Run, which stretches down West Seventh Street from Spruce to Harrison.

Rocky Mountain Too High
Leadville

Leadville gets a lot of mileage out of its ranking as highest incorporated city in the country. Doctors come to do studies (one doc in the 1960s even catheterized a bunch of local high school kids just to see if they suffered any pulmonary hypertension), partyers come for the alcohol buzz (a two-ounce shot of Jack Daniels goes twice as far in Leadville as it does in, say, San Diego), the high school basketball team likes to psyche out opponents by setting up oxygen tanks near their benches, and the chamber of commerce proudly touts the "highest city" distinction in all its literature. Of course, the Leadville

★ ★

chamber is probably the only one anywhere that also offers a health proviso to potential tourists: "Stay at 5,000 feet for a day or two before coming. Get extra rest, drink more water, and avoid alcoholic beverages, caffeine, and salty food."

It's just that there's one little catch with the ranking: There are two other municipalities (both in Colorado, of course) that are higher according to the official USGS contour maps. Alma, which rings in at 10,355 feet, and Montezuma, which is perched at 10,335, are a couple hundred feet higher than Leadville at 10,152. If you want to get nitpicky, you can make a case that Leadville is the highest city since Alma and Montezuma are towns, but incorporated municipalities nonetheless.

But no matter who is higher, Leadvillians will always get a big kick out of a certain World War II movie in which the squad captain tells his bomber crew that they're going to have to wear oxygen masks because "we're going to 10,200 feet."

Night of the Living Dead
Leadville

Lots of teens spend Halloween in graveyards. It's a ritual as common as proms and homecoming dances. But how many honorable judges do you know who spend their Halloweens in cemeteries, particularly haunted cemeteries from the 1870s?

In Leadville, there's a U.S. municipal judge named Neil V. Reynolds who not only goes ghost-busting himself each Hallowed Eve, but also takes visitors as well on lantern-lit tours of Lake County's Evergreen Cemetery. Wearing a black top hat and long black cape, Judge Reynolds recounts tales of early Leadville residents whose remains lie interred beneath markers of granite, metal, and even petrified wood.

Among those laid to rest in Evergreen Cemetery are "Pony" Nelson, a prostitute who worked the local brothels, then nicknamed "riding academies"; the now-markerless grave of one John W. Booth, who claimed to be the cousin of the assassin of President Abraham

Lincoln; and "Texas Jack" Omohundro, who guided Buffalo Bill and performed at Leadville's Chestnut Street Theater before succumbing to pneumonia at the age of thirty-nine. In September 1908 Buffalo Bill Cody paid tribute to his old friend by organizing a memorial service at the Evergreen Cemetery, which was attended by his entire Wild West circus troupe.

The Evergreen Cemetery is located at the northwestern edge of Leadville, at the intersection of Tenth and James Streets. The tours, which take place every Halloween, can be arranged by calling (800) 933-3901. Fee.

Leadville's resident ghostbuster, the Honorable Judge Neil V. Reynolds.
Marcia Martinek, *Herald Democrat*

★ ★

Practice Makes Perfect

Leadville

"Ah, pardon me for noticing, but doesn't the calendar say it's September?"

"Yep, September 17."

"But isn't that green all those people are wearing? Aren't those shamrocks? Isn't that an Irish bagpipe band marching down Harrison Avenue?"

"Yep."

"But why are they all saying 'Top of the morning to you' and 'Erin go braless'? Isn't this fall color season?"

"Yep." Long pause. "Oh, I get it. You're from out of town."

Leadville may be the only place on the planet that has a bigger rehearsal parade for St. Paddy's Day than the real deal. Leadville's St. Patrick's Day Practice Parade, held every September since 1979, makes perfect sense to natives. The weather's perfect, green clothing contrasts nicely with the yellow aspens, and besides, the bagpipers need off-season practice. Plus in March, when everybody else is eating corned beef and cabbage, Leadville, the highest incorporated city in the country, is usually covered with snow.

Not that Leadvillians don't also gamely stride down Harrison Avenue on March 17. Even in the worst of weather, Judge Neil V. Reynolds and cronies Ed Kerrigan and Jim O'Neal (aka the Greater Leadville Hibernian Mining and Marching Society) lead the annual Leadville St. Patrick's Day Parade. It's just that few spectators share their enthusiasm plus, as Reynolds points out, it's next to impossible to play the bagpipes when they're frozen.

Hence, the Practice Parade six months earlier. Starting at noon sharp, at the corner of Ninth and Harrison Avenues, the Greater Leadville Hibernian Mining and Marching Society once again lead the parade. Only in September, they're followed by an exuberant contingent of green-clad locals, vintage fire trucks, kilted step dancers, green automobiles, and at least three bagpipe-and-drum ensembles

Top of the September morning to you.
Marcia Martinek, *Herald Democrat*

from Denver, Fort Collins, and other Colorado communities.

After entertaining the crowd for an hour or so in front of the courthouse (and occasionally being asked to officiate a wedding), Judge Reynolds with his watch fob, carved walking stick, and natty derby, proceeds, Pied Piper–like, along with the bagpipes, the drums, and the dancers, to Leadville's 1879 Silver Dollar Saloon.

★ ★

But Where's Cartman and Mr. Hanky?
South Park City in Fairplay

Trey Parker and Matt Stone put South Park on the national map, but the real South Park, an old mining town that rests smack dab in the center of Colorado, was here long before Cartman, Kenny, Chef, and Mr. Hanky. Unlike the irreverent TV series, the real South

A town with "damned few mosquitoes."
South Park Historical Foundation

Park has wooden sidewalks, an authentic one-room schoolhouse, a drugstore that sells rock candy, and a chamber of commerce that has been laughing all the way to the bank ever since the foulmouthed animated series debuted in 1997. In fact, according to the South Park Chamber of Commerce Web site, they're even thinking of naming something in the restored mining town after Parker and Stone, to thank them for all they've done for the little burg.

And, as it says on the chamber Web site, "South Park is paradise compared to most of the rest of the country. We have no fleas, no snakes, no termites, no cockroaches, no fire ants, no alligators, no poison ivy, no tornadoes or hurricanes or humidity, and damned few mosquitoes."

For more information, contact the South Park Historical Foundation, P.O. Box 634, Fairplay, CO 80440; (719) 836-2387; www.south parkcity.org.

Splat!

For a while, the little town of Twin Lakes near Leadville seemed to have solved the problem of what to do with all those extra tomatoes gardeners end up with in late August. It hosted the one and only Twin Lakes Tomato War. The population of 20 swelled to 500 or 600 folks who came to lob juicy, ripe tomatoes at each other. This was before Leadville had a police officer, which is how, I suppose, they got away with it. Alas, the Twin Lakes Tomato War was disbanded.

6

Crested Butte

If this were a book about familiarity or mediocrity, I'd have to skip Crested Butte altogether. Oh, I'm sure one of its 1,500 residents might squeak by as normal, but, for the most part, this is a town with people and traditions and festivals unlike any other. That's why it's one of two mountain towns in Colorado that merits its own chapter.

Locals have names like Lipstick and Tuck, Cricket and Rat, Glo and Tree. The only chain in town is on a bicycle. And everything, from the end of ski season to the reopening of an old museum, is an excuse for a party. Or a parade. Or a costume ball. Oftentimes, all three. Name one other place where you can find an honorary king hoisting a toilet plunger scepter brimming with beer.

Although it's not in the city code (the city code stipulates such things as "lights must be dim enough that every child under twelve can see the stars"), it's common knowledge that a basic requirement of being a Buttian, as they call themselves, is to own at least one costume. An ape suit or a Martha Stewart mask is acceptable. Purple wigs, feathery boas, or a Mr. Peanut hat will also work.

Crested Butte has way too many annual events requiring mandatory costuming not to have at least one in the back of your closet. Take the Clunker Crit during Fat Tire Bike Week, for example. That's when locals ride paperboy-style bikes in little red devil tails or Attila the Hun costumes. Or the Al Johnson Memorial Uphill/Downhill Ski Race, when

★ ★

locals telemark up and down steep slopes dressed as pink fluorescent bunnies or six-packs of beer. Then there's the Red Lady Ball, the Black and White Ball, the Fourth of July parade (skunk cabbage is a popular costume for that event), and, of course, the two bookends of ski season, Vinotok and Flauschink, that simply cannot be attended without proper costuming. Oh yeah, and the ability to polka.

In fact, the only event where you can get away without a costume is the last day of ski season, and that's only because everyone skis in the buff.

Any excuse for a competition will do, be it who can shake their groove thing in the wildest, reddest outfit to who can pull the heaviest cement block on the back of their old Schwinn. When it's your birthday, you get your name in the paper, and if you stick around long enough, you'll eventually be appointed Flauschink King or Vinotok Green Man or the Red Lady for the High Country Citizens' Alliance.

There's a glacial valley outside Crested Butte called Oh-Be-Joyful. It could easily be the town motto. If anything does go wrong, Buttians write it on a piece of paper, stick it in an effigy of a grump, and burn it all to hell. They know it doesn't pay to fret or really do much of anything but revel in the two magnificent mountain ranges between which they're wedged.

★ ★

Two-Bike Garage

Nobody in Crested Butte has one bike. It'd be like having one glove or one ski. Two bikes is the bare minimum. Most have three or four. Naturally, you have a mountain bike. There are far too many back-country trails not to. Your mountain bike is frequently worth more than your car.

But you also have what's known as a "townie" bike. This is what you ride to the Eldo or the Wooden Nickel. Usually it has bells and

"Townies" competed in the world's first mountain bike tour.
Beth Buehler, Gunnison–Crested Butte Tourism Association

streamers, maybe a bumper sticker or a basket to carry your beer or a tube to haul your skis. It resembles a bike the newspaper delivery boy used to ride. Those who don't call them townies call them "klunkers." They're usually made from spare parts, maybe the frame from an old Schwinn Varsity, a rusted rim from a JC Higgins.

The advantage of a townie is nobody in their right mind would ever dream of stealing one. It'd be like confiscating someone else's fingerprint. In fact, locals find each other at night by tracking down their townies. To wit: "There's Lipstick's townie. She must be at the Timberline."

During Crested Butte's Fat Tire Bike Week, the oldest mountain bike festival in the world, there's often a Clunker Crit, a 12-mile townie bike race down mountains and winding through Crested Butte's historic alleys. Bikes are decorated, costumes are worn, and adult beverages are consumed.

For information about Fat Tire Bike Week, call the Crested Butte Chamber of Commerce at (800) 545-4505.

Waiting for Godot

As long waits go, John Plute, a Crested Butte hunter who had to wait sixty-two years before getting recognition for his "world's largest elk rack," may take the prize. But we'll tell you for sure in another hundred years.

In the fall of 1899, Plute, who was hunting Dark Canyon of Anthracite Creek, came across a monster bull elk. He managed to get a bead on the behemoth, shoot him, and drag home enough elk meat to get him and a small army through the long winter. He also had the foresight to keep the 52-inch rack. It collected dust in a shed for a few years, then hung on the wall of a Crested Butte saloon for another sixty before Ed and Tony Rozman decided it should be measured by the Boone and Crockett Club, a veritable "who's who" when it comes to big-game records.

On March 19, 1961, Plute finally got the recognition he deserved,

Rack and roll.
Gunnison–Crested Butte Tourism Association

earning the record for the world's largest elk he'd shot sixty-two years earlier with a 30-40 Krag rifle. In 1997, long after Plute had traveled to that happy hunting ground in the sky, a film was made about his legendary hunt. But alas, Plute's record was broken the next year when an Arizona elk measured in at a measly ¼-inch longer.

The prize-winning rack is on display at the Crested Butte Visitor's Center at 601 Elk Avenue.

Tuck Everlasting

Not many sixty-five-year-old men are asked to pose nude. But then not many sixty-five-year-old men have a tattoo on the top of their head or muscles that Arnold Schwarzenegger would gladly give up his California governorship for. If you're from the Butte, you already know I'm talking about Tuck, a former New York narcotics and vice cop who has a black belt in Shotokan karate, an acting gift that has won him parts in nineteen Shakespearean plays, and a charm that has won over the hearts of every adult, kid, and dog in town. Tuck (like Madonna and Cher, he's known by only one name) is as popular around town as free skiing was in the 1990s.

When Paul Hooge approached Tuck about being the first in a series of nude ski posters (after all, it's one of many sports Crested Butte is notorious for), he gladly signed on. It certainly wasn't the first time he'd bared his behind. As a supervisor for Mountain Express, the free local bus company, he organizes what's known in town as the Moon Bus. On the last day of ski season, locals crowd into Tuck's bus so they can line up along the windows and "moon" all the restaurants.

A Vietnam vet, Tuck says Crested Butte gave him back his life. He came to the quirky town in 1973 a bitter and broken man. Between Vietnam, working the '60s race riots, and losing one of his three kids, Tuck was confused and lonely when he came to the area for a fishing getaway. "I felt like I'd stepped inside heaven," he says.

Today, he's a fulfilled and happy man. He's part of the East River Free Trappers, a historical reenactment group; he hunts with a bow and arrow; he acts in local productions; and in the summer, he lives in a tepee.

Surprisingly, Tuck Naked, the black-and-white poster that can be found in several area art galleries, isn't Tuck's first poster. Look back at the 1964 Summer Olympic Games poster and you'll see Tuck right there in the second row. He ran track and field for the U.S. team.

Tuck Naked can be found by appointment at the Lucille Lucas Gallery, 318 Elk Avenue; phone (970) 349-1903 or visit www.lucillelucasgallery.com.

On a Bright Cloud of Music

The old joke is that if you want to make it in business, you'd better learn to golf. If you want to make it in Crested Butte, you'd better learn to polka. And fast. Although coal smoke no longer drifts into the night air, accordion music still does, and usually it's accompanied by folks of all ages stomping their heels to the 2/4 beat.

Many of Crested Butte's early Croats and Slovenians are dying out, but there's a whole new generation of Buttian polka dancers who hoof it up at the town's many ethnic-inspired festivals. In fact, don't even think about running for Red Lady or Green Man or Queen of Flauschink if you can't tell the difference between Polish-style, Slovenian-style, Conjunto-style, and Dutchman-style polka.

Retired air force pilot Pete Dunda, who has a three-piece polka band in the area, says he's busier than a one-armed concertina player. "We could play a gig every weekend if we wanted to," he says. He takes his responsibility as the area torch carrier of polka music quite seriously. He and his wife will teach anybody who calls how to dance the folksy 2/4 beat. And if you long to know the history of polka, just ask.

Dunda is a walking encyclopedia of anything having to do with accordions, an instrument he learned to play when he was five, and all things polka. He says the polka has been in Crested Butte since the mining town's inception. "Entertainment in those days was scarce," he says. "The immigrants had to entertain themselves. They brought the accordions and the polka over from the old country."

Two for the Price of One

Buttians are nothing if not resourceful. They've got a wine bar that doubles as a designer furnishings store. It's called Princess Western Design Company by day and by night Princess Wine Bar, a *Wine Spectator* award–winning establishment. There's an old hardware store that doubles as a museum and a Mountain Bike Hall of Fame. The museum, which still has the coal stove and all the original cases of hardware, is called the Mountain Heritage Museum and tells the

★ ★

story of the early mines and the folks who have kept Crested Butte alive over the years. The Mountain Bike Hall of Fame shows off classic bikes, early photos, and mementos of the homegrown sport of mountain biking. Over the years, it has also been a blacksmith shop, a gas station, and an auto supply store.

And there's a lodge less than 300 feet from the ski lift that doubles as a museum of skiing. Hooge Haus (aka Ski History Inn) was started by Paul and Kathy Hooge, who have been skiing and collecting ski memorabilia since childhood.

The Hooge Haus/Ski History Inn is located at 18 Castle Road, Mt. Crested Butte; phone (800) 349-1601. The Princess Wine Bar/Western Design Company is at 218 Elk Avenue; (970) 349-0210 or 329-5188. The Mountain Heritage Museum and the Mountain Bike Hall of Fame are at Fourth and Elk Avenues; (970) 349-1880; or visit the hall of fame's Web site at www.mtnbikehalloffame.com.

Evel Knievel for Mayor

Most politicians win votes by shaking hands, knocking on doors. But Alan Bernholtz, the current mayor of Crested Butte, was elected partly for his unique ability to ski jump through a hoop of flaming fire. While his mayoral platform was certainly analyzed, many voters marked his name on the ballot simply for his unique ability to inject creativity and pyrotechnics into the town's many parades down Elk Avenue.

Until that fateful day eight years ago when Bernholtz asked a friend to create a ski jump on the back of his Suburban, most of the floats in the Mardi Gras parade were, well, ho-hum. "There might be an H&H Towing Truck or a van with the company's name on the side," Bernholtz says. "I wanted to do something that was fun, something that wasn't commercialized."

Indeed, Bernholtz's first entry in the float competition was anything but commercialized. Death-defying might be a better description. He attached two trailers to his Suburban, put a band on one, a kicker on both, then lit the jumps on fire while he rode through town clearing the gap.

★ ★

Although the grand prize he won (a $50 bar tab) wasn't much to write home about, the glory and the sheer preposterousness of jumping back and forth over two 55-gallon drums of flames hooked him. "I mean, who wouldn't want to jump through fire?" he asks with a completely straight face.

Now, rarely a parade goes by when the mayor and the owner of Crested Butte Mountain Guides doesn't enter something. One year, he had a Slip 'n Slide. Another time, there was a zip line that dropped into an 80-gallon horse tank. And while no one has offered to join him on the 17-foot jump through flaming hoops yet, there are always takers for the Slip 'n Slide.

"That year, this sixty-three-year-old guy who works for the city was following our float the whole parade. People dressed like ballerinas,

Oh Mr. Mayor, when you're done jumping through that ring of fire,
I have a bill for you to sign.
Chris Ladoulis/Crested Butte Mountain Resort

★ ★

Fred Flintstone, and Richard Nixon were jumping on the float partaking of the Slip 'n Slide. Finally, he couldn't resist. He gets up there in his suit and tie and goes for it," Bernholtz says.

You might think elaborate floats such as Bernholtz's Bizzaro World Float take months of planning. After all, look at the Rose Bowl Parade.

Nope.

"We just get up the day of the parade and throw something together. I call my friends, who come over to my house with screw guns, mint julep fixings, and attitude," he says.

The winning float (the ski jump) took all of three hours.

To contact Alan's Crested Butte Mountain Guides, call (970) 349-5430, or visit on the Web at www.crestedbutteguides.com.

Lab Rats

Forget every stereotype you've ever had about science labs. The Rocky Mountain Biological Laboratory at Gothic, just 7 miles up the mountain from Crested Butte, defies everything you've ever thought about science labs—that they're cramped, filled with test tubes and guys in white jackets, and located within the strict confines of academia.

Confining is the last word you'd ever think of when visiting this lab. Not only is the "office" located 9,500 feet above sea level with views that make any seeing person weak in the knees, but many of its research facilities are housed in weathered wood cabins from the silver mining days.

At one time Gothic was in danger of becoming just another Colorado ghost town. Dr. John C. Johnson, a biology professor at Western State College, decided that since the area gets higher than normal rainfall and has an astounding variety of plants, insects, and birds, he'd buy the whole town and use it as a research station. That was back in 1928. Today, up to 160 biologists from all the prominent universities come to the 245-acre Rocky Mountain Biological Laboratory to research, write, and, yes, relax. RMBL's specialty, of course, is understanding and protecting high-altitude and alpine ecosystems. It's

★ ★

known in the science biz as being one of the world's largest and oldest independent field stations.

Every summer, Gothic hosts scientists from around the world, some
of whom have ongoing thirty-year projects, and the scientists in turn
are nice enough to give tours to laypeople like me. They even offer
kids' nature camps. As for that stereotype about scientists having no
sense of humor, you should see the skunk cabbage costumes they
come up with every summer for Crested Butte's wacky Fourth of July
parade.

For more information about Rocky Mountain Biological Laboratory
and the organization's summer activities, write RMBL at P.O. Box 519,
Crested Butte, CO 81224; call (970) 349-7231, or visit www.rmbl.org.

Ghost town lab.
Gunnison–Crested Butte Tourism Association

Blue, Blue, My Vein Is Blue

Until 1834, when painters figured out how to reproduce the color ultramarine by roasting kaolin clay, sodium sulfate, and charcoal, the gemstone lapis lazuli was used to make the deep, rich pigment in the great masters' paintings of the Virgin Mary's robes. Still today, the stone that's mined in the Hindu Kush Mountains of Afghanistan is pulverized and added to oil used to restore some of the famous paintings of the Renaissance and Middle Ages.

So why, you're undoubtedly wondering, am I discussing a rare and precious gemstone from Afghanistan in a book about Colorado? Well, here's the thing most people don't realize: North Italian Mountain near Crested Butte has an outstanding vein of lapis lazuli. There's even a mine of the opaque blue gemstone in a remote 12,700-foot-high valley along upper Cement Creek.

Although the Afghans have been mining their lapis for 6,000 years, selling it to the Egyptians who used it to make jewelry and talismans, the Indians who put it in the Taj Mahal, and the Chinese who used it in screens, nobody knew the Colorado deposit was there until 1940, when Gunnison character Carl Anderson discovered it on his mountain property. Known as "The Blue Wrinkle," his makeshift mine sported the following sign: THIS PROPERTY BELONGS TO A MADMAN. HE'S A DEAD SHOT. NO DIGGING. For a while, the Colorado lapis was brought down and sold in gift stores in Crested Butte and Gunnison. Some claimed it even cured snakebites. But lately the Colorado lapis movement has ground to a halt, and the rumor that Afghanistan is the only place to get the rare gemstone has once again gained momentum.

★ ★

Flush Hour Traffic

Don't feel bad if you can't pronounce Crested Butte's annual end-of-ski-season party. The word *Flauschink* (pronounced FLOSH-ink), after all, has not yet made it into *Webster's* and is not a household name that rolls fluidly off most tongues.

But who really cares what you call it as long as you know the following five essential facts: (1) royalty will preside, (2) adult beverages will be consumed, (3) bands will play, (4) polkas will be danced, and (5) a parade that has been compared to the Rose Bowl's will head down Elk Avenue.

The royalty I mentioned are the Flauschink king and queen, who preside over the parade (not only do they ride on the lead float, but they do so wielding scepters made from toilet plungers), have personal poems written about their glory, and get a lifetime pass to ride a Flauschink float, though after their first year of Miss America–like honor, they're relegated to the "Has-Beens" float.

By now, there are plenty of has-beens. Flauschink has been going strong since 1969, when George Sibley, a professor of journalism and environmental studies at Western State, decided that ski season, instead of going out with a whimper, should go out with a bang.

Although he admits the invented word (could it be Slavic for "flushing out winter"?) might get him in trouble with the Slavic National Union, Sibley hopes it also honors Crested Butte's Slavic forefathers, who knew how to drink slivovitz, eat kielbasa, and stomp their heels with the best of them.

Parts of Elk Avenue are blocked off, and a huge movie screen is mounted on the front of Bacchanale Restaurant for ski movies, including those filmed by local companies Matchstick Productions and Two Plank Productions.

For more information about Flaush, flush, flash, whatever it's called, call (800) 814-8893, or check out Crested Butte's fantastic Web site at www.gunnisoncrestedbutte.com.

Wait till Bogner hears about this!
Crested Butte Mountain Resort

Wait a Minute, Aren't You Supposed to Ski Downhill?

Nobody's admitting it, but Al Johnson, the poster boy for the zaniest ski race in the world, was probably the guy the U.S. Postal Service was referring to in its famous slogan: "Neither snow nor rain nor heat nor gloom of night. . . ."

Johnson was the mailman for Crested Butte and surrounding mining towns in the late nineteenth century. Most of his 17-mile route took place at 9,000 feet and involved snowed-in cabins, 25-pound mail sacks, and terrain that today would be strictly verboten by the ski patrol.

Even though the diehard mailman came in second in the first ski race ever held in Gunnison Valley (Presidents' Day, 1886), Johnson and his intrepid mail route was the obvious choice as namesake for the annual race.

The Al Johnson Memorial Uphill/Downhill Telemark Ski Race (or AJ, as it's affectionately known; New Belgium Brewing Company even brews an AJ beer) has been taking place annually since 1974 and involves hundreds of skiers in, well, let's just call them unusual costumes. Just know that if you enter, you'll be vying against gorillas, Statues of Liberties, leprechauns, nuns, the Skippy Peanut Butter Man, Martha Stewart in black-and-white prison duds, and, one year, even Jesus carrying a 6-foot cross.

The unique race begins just below the headwall on Mount Crested Butte and climbs 600 vertical feet to the ridge of North Face. If that doesn't do you in, you're then required to plunge 1,200 feet down what can only be officially classified as double-black diamonds.

The good news is that "every competitor wins something." The bad news (as if the 600-foot vertical climb and the double-black diamonds weren't enough) is that the only allowed ski is telemark. Yes, that's the ski where your heel wobbles freely without binding.

For more info about the Al Johnson Memorial Uphill/Downhill Telemark Ski Race, contact P.O. Box 208, Crested Butte, CO 81224; (970) 349-5210; www.aljohnsonrace.com.

Matchstick Men

Forget Hollywood. If you're looking for action and adventure ski films, look no further than Crested Butte, home of Matchstick Productions, the leader in extreme sports filmmaking. The innovative company was started inadvertently in 1991 by Steve Winter, who after finally despairing of ever starring in a ski movie, decided to make one instead. He enrolled in a video production class at the Seattle Art Institute, but at the last minute, he decided his tuition money would be better spent on a used 16 mm camera and a road trip that took him to Jackson Hole, Alta, and Crested Butte in a '73 Volkswagen van. It was a wise decision. In fact, the end result, the fifteen-minute classic *Nachos and Fear*, was shot and wrapped before the class had even ended.

With $150 left to his name, Winter talked a high school classmate and old ski buddy, Murray Wais, into going with him to the Las Vegas Ski and Snowboard Convention. They borrowed Wais's girlfriend's car, slept in hotel lobbies, and spent the rest of the time passing out the fifty copies of *Nachos and Fear* they could afford to make.

Luckily, one of the fifty copies impelled ski mogul K2 to hire the ballsy filmmakers to film a product video. They began producing ski movies out of their rented A-frame house in Crested Butte. The rest, as they say, is history.

Matchstick Productions (so named because they wanted to "ignite the flame under the ski industry's ass") has gone on to produce dozens of feature-length films, including *The Hedonist, Sick Sense, Ski Movie,* and *Global Storming,* the first film Winter did after breaking two vertebrae in a plane crash over the Chilean Andes. www.skimovie .com.

How the Grump Stole Vinotok

Usually, when you hear there's going to be a Passion play, you think of Easter and crosses and gory endings. In Crested Butte, the annual Passion play is held not in the spring, but in the fall; crucifies not a half-naked guy with a beard, but a 20-foot homemade metal-and-cloth "Grump" that is ceremoniously stuffed full of last year's complaints; and the ending, instead of being gory, is as happy as they come. Besides the Grump, whose head is chopped off before being burned in a huge bonfire, Crested Butte's Passion play involves a virile Green Man, a pregnant Harvest Mother, an Earth Dragon, Sir Hapless, and a whole cast of maidens, torch bearers, fairies, and straw boys.

The Saturday night Passion play is the final episode of Crested Butte's annual Vinotok Festival, a medieval fall celebration that takes place on the autumnal equinox. This storytelling festival usually kicks off Thursday night with Liar's Night, when locals show up at the Eldo to outdo each other with tall tales. On Friday night there's a Harvest Festival Feast and polka dancing, and Saturday, of course, is the procession, trial, and burning of the Grump. Children make grump boxes

★ ★

Vinotok is the only community celebration in America that uses its streets as a series of stages and turns its central crossroads into a two-story bonfire.
Jane Chaney/Gunnison–Crested Butte Tourism Association

that are placed around town prior to Vinotok so that both locals and visitors can write down any bad karma they want to burn away for the upcoming year. On that night a single man is named as the "Green Man," and it is his job to represent harvest and fertility and slash the head off that horrible old Grump.

The word *vinotok* means fall wine festival and was started in Crested Butte some twenty years ago by Marcie Telander to celebrate the town's Eastern European heritage. By recording and honoring stories from the old-timers, Telander was able to bring a divided community back together.

For more information about Vinotok, call Molly Murfee at (970) 349-0947.

Brave Nude World

Back when Crested Butte offered free no-strings-attached lift tickets to anybody willing to figure out a way to get to the remote but remarkable ski resort, it got lots of media exposure. I mean, everyone from *Ski* magazine to the *New York Times* to the *Tokyo Daily* ran a story on this crazy but effective marketing scheme. Heck, how long has it been since anything was given away free?

But the exposure I'm about to bring up is of a different color, an exposure that sometimes results in uncomfortable sunburns and, in the case of Crested Butte, annoying boycotts and/or a few thrown beer bottles and police arrests.

Our story begins twenty-five-some years ago when Crested Butte was an almost-forgotten former coal mining town at the end of a road less traveled. The locals who liked it that way (who needs CNN and throngs of Texans?) celebrated the last day of ski season by wearing what some might call an unconventional ski outfit. Yep, they wore nothing but their birthday suits (oh, well, right, they also had on ski boots)—on the lifts, down the mountain, and even on mountain restaurant decks.

Like all long-standing traditions, it started with one person, a random streaker who stuffed his parka and ski pants in his daypack and flashed his way down the mountain. By 1994 Crested Butte's Naked Day was common ski lore knowledge. No less an authority on nudity than *Playboy* magazine billed it as the place America goes to ski naked.

Although Crested Butte Mountain Resort never sanctioned Naked Day (in fact, they had the nerve to officially ban nudity from all lifts and resort-owned restaurants after the word got out), the reputation had already stuck. By 1997 Naked Day had snowballed into a no-holds-barred bender with indie cult singer-guitarist Juliana Hatfield playing on the deck of Rafters for thousands of fans, some clothed, some not.

But then a right-wing county commissioner from Colorado Springs boycotted a government conference that was to be held in Crested Butte, and all hell broke loose. Town leaders and the conference organizers, I'm proud to report, didn't give in, noting to anyone who asked that "Crested Butte is the kind of community in which how people choose to ski is considered none of the government's business."

However, the next year the hundreds of naked skiers were joined by thousands of gawkers in clothes, which eventually led to vandalism, disorderly conduct, and a bunch of beer bottles being bandied about. Although the naked skiers shouldered the blame, it should be noted that the skiers sans clothes had been there for decades, while the clothed skiers were the new variable in the mix.

Nowadays there are signs warning potential nudists about the consequences. But every year on Crested Butte's very last ski day, there's still one last Jonathan Livingston Seagull who steps out of the V formation, sheds his duds, and whoops down the mountain in nothing but resplendent glory.

Take That, Aspen

As rumor has it, a bunch of high rollers from Aspen rode over Pearl Pass one day in the 1970s to thumb their noses at the little backwater on CO 135. They parked their big fancy-schmancy motorcycles outside the Grubstake Saloon, one of only two bars at the time, hogging most of the unpaved parking.

Well, as far as a group of local rowdies were concerned, a counter-assault was the only reasonable response. So one September morning in 1976, fourteen Crested Butte cyclists took off on their one-speed clunkers, heading over the same pass into Aspen. It took them two days to crest the 12,700-foot Pearl Pass, but once they did, they wasted no time parking their bikes in front of the tony Hotel Jerome and launching one hell of a raucous party.

This all-in-fun vendetta is credited as being the very first mountain bike tour, and the epic seven-hour adventure, now known in riding circles as the Pearl Pass Tour, is the longest-running organized bike tour in the world. It's still held every September.

For details about this historic bike tour, contact the Mountain Bike

Hall of Fame, P.O. Box 845, Crested Butte, CO 81224; (970) 349-6817; www.mtnbikehalloffame.com.

Flower Power

In Crested Butte people go plum crazy for wildflowers. They make beer out of them, they flavor ice cream with them, they use them to heal everything from car sickness to arthritis. And every July, the folks of Crested Butte host a huge weeklong festival in honor of wildflowers.

Held for some twenty years, the Crested Butte Wildflower Festival features 170 events ranging from identification hikes to wildflower tea parties to workshops on how to make beer out of wildflowers. Let's just say the possibilities are endless—whether you want to see wildflowers, smell wildflowers, touch wildflowers, or even eat wildflowers, this festival has it all.

In 1989 the Colorado legislature designated Crested Butte as the wildflower capital of Colorado, an honor the town has used to great effect.

Crested Butte Wildflower Festival, P.O. Box 216, Crested Butte, CO 81224; (970) 349-2571; www.crestedbuttewildflowerfestival.com.

Chrome, Sweet Chrome

Next to skiing and, oh yeah, mountain biking, the most popular sport in Crested Butte may be bench sitting. Locals "coffee up," a term that in the Butte means grabbing an extra-strong java; finding a bench on Elk Avenue; and proceeding to yell at speeders, wave at friends, and chat up anyone interesting who happens to mosey by.

By far the most interesting benches in town are those constructed by chrome sculptor Sean Guerrero, who also built the giant dragon and medieval knight on the south end of town. The Guerrero benches, built from old auto bumpers and other unwanted metals from vintage cars, can be found on Elk Avenue. Guerrero was a local

★ ★

Life's a bench.
Beth Buehler/Gunnison–Crested Butte Tourism Association

for many years, spending summers in Crested Butte and winters in the Bordeaux region of France.

Once an industrial welder, Guerrero began welding small sculptures in his spare time. His work started selling (Kirk Douglas and Jack Palance are two of his customers), and in 1981 he switched to fulltime sculpting. Besides benches, Guerrero creates usable furniture, wind-blown sculpture, skaters, robots, and aliens and likes to use discarded appliances, light bulbs, and anything else cast off by society. The downside to metal fabrication, Guerrero says, is the finished sculptures weigh on average at least a ton.

License to Chill

These days, houses are made from straw bales, tires, and concrete blocks. But Crested Butte leads the nation in an entirely different architectural phenomenon: buildings constructed from license plates. To be editorially correct, I should probably say buildings sided with license plates. Underneath, the unique Crested Butte architecture is regular frame construction with gabled roofs, but the siding includes dented, curling license plates from every decade since Colorado started issuing them in 1913. Before that, you got a number and made your own.

There's a two-bedroom, two-bath rental house on Fourth Street, just off Elk Avenue, the main drag, that's covered with license plates and a popular coffee shop next door called Camp 4 Coffee that also features the unique architectural style.

Architectural license.
Gunnison–Crested Butte Tourism Association

★ ★

This breakout style began soon after 1949, when Jessie Mae Richardson, the wife of a miner, began nailing old license plates to an old coal shed that her daughter, Mildred, and son-in-law, Lyle McNeil, moved from Big Mine Hill to Crested Butte. No one knows for sure why Jessie Mae began creating that first folk art installation. Maybe it was nerves. Her husband, Ben, was a fire boss at Floresta, the country's highest mine, and his job was to go in first and check for toxic gases and rockfalls. Or maybe it was repressed inner artistic urgings.

This much we do know: People from all over the world send their license plates to Al and Wythina Smith, owners of Camp 4 Coffee, who faithfully save them and, when there's time, screw them to Camp 4 Coffee's three other locations at Painter Boy Shack and Crested Butte South.

We also know this: Crested Butte is not a safe place for the 3,000 members of the Automobile License Plate Collectors. The stellar examples of antique license plates from every decade are just too big a temptation.

The License Plate Rental House is located at 404 Elk Avenue, Crested Butte (if you're interested in staying there, call Texan Bob Hunt at 214-824-5750). Camp 4 Coffee, which locals consistently vote as the best java in town (its motto is "Third World Technology, First World Flavor"), is located at 401½ Elk Avenue; (970) 349-2500; www.camp4coffee.com.

Bench Warmer

The world's largest bench can be found at the top of Painter Boy Lift at Crested Butte Mountain Resort. It sits outside Camp 4 Coffee and can seat up to forty-five folks, probably more if they're not wearing ski parkas.

Al Smith, the owner of Camp 4 Coffee, who is known around Crested Butte as a world-class scrounger (when people have something to get rid of, they call Al), had the monstrous bench built after he'd heard this huge spruce log was going to be thrown away or chopped into firewood. Not under his watch.

The world's largest bench is a nice piece of furniture, no doubt, but it has its drawbacks. For one thing, it takes a 4-foot crane and a long trailer to even budge it. It weighs 2,200 pounds, and Al has had to move it twice—when he rescued it from the house where it was discarded and again when its spot in downtown Crested Butte was replaced with a rock wall.

"We like to think we're in the coffee business, but we're really in the bench-sitting business," Al says. "You put up a comfortable bench, people sit down, and before long they wish they had a cup of coffee."

Living on Red Alone

Forget the tuxedos, burn the long gowns. For Crested Butte's annual Red Lady Ball, the mandatory dress code is that whatever you wear— be it long johns, choir gown, or ski parka—has to be bright red.

Wear it flamboyantly enough and you might even be crowned the community's reigning "Red Lady," a coveted position that has caused more than a few catfights. Over the years, winners have donned every-thing from red vinyl miniskirts to red sequined boas. And if you can find

What some people won't do to save a mountain.
Nancy Wick/Gunnison–Crested Butte Tourism Association

★ ★

.a red ruffled tuxedo shirt a la the 1970s or red fishnets, all the better.

The Red Lady Ball started back in 1978, when the community decided to take on a mining conglomerate named AMAX, who thought it would be in their best financial interests to destroy one of the valley's most gorgeous mountains, Mount Emmons, or the Red Lady, as it's affectionately known around town. The community determined that letting AMAX waltz right in and glibly mine their beloved backcountry ski area was not a prudent decision. So they formed an organization named HCCA (High Country Citizens' Alliance) and launched the Red Lady Ball, a fund-raiser that still attracts hundreds.

The criterion for becoming the Red Lady, who is known as the spiritual soul of the community, has changed. It has gone from fancy dance moves and bawdy costumes to being nominated by the community for your "dedication to the environment." Not that contestants don't continue to shake their groove thing, it's just that it's now in the name of preservation.

Royal responsibilities during a Red Lady reign include entering the Al Johnson Race and waving at the Fourth of July and Flauschink parades. But oh, the perks! The winner gets a crown passed on from Lady to Lady (it's a motley conglomeration of red fabric, rhinestone brooches, pearls, tiny silk roses, and sparkles) for the year of her (or his) reign, a fairy princess necklace (that the winner gets to keep), and a box of red items that include a red biking shirt, a red mini dress, a red silk shirt, red "I Dream of Jeannie" pants, red T-shirts, and red ski poles. Over the years, two men have stolen the title: Bill Smith (Red Lady 1983) and Scott Yost (Red Lady 2003).

For more information about the Red Lady Ball, call the HCCA at (970) 349-7104, or check out their Web site at www.hccaonline.org.

Deep Doo Doo

Unlike Gays, Illinois, which made its two-story outhouse an official state tourism spot, the folks of Crested Butte barely blink an eye when you mention theirs. In fact, ask locals where's it's located, and

The last of several two-story outhouses in Crested Butte.
Gunnison–Crested Butte Tourism Association

they'll probably just shrug. It's not that they don't know (it's right behind the old Masonic Hall, if you must know), it's just that searching for it is a good excuse to explore the rest of the town.

As the story goes, Crested Butte's two-story outhouse (the only one of a half dozen or so two-story outhouses that are still in operation) was built before snow-removing equipment solved the nasty problem of 10-foot snowdrifts. The first-floor hole worked great in the summer, but come winter, when Crested Butte gets as much as 30 feet of snow, the outhouse was what you might call inaccessible in emergencies. An innovative carpenter, who understood the adage When you gotta go, you gotta go, simply added a second tier to the outhouse with a separate entrance leading out from the upper floor.

For a while, Crested Butte had a second two-story outhouse. It was located behind the city hall. However, when the marshal's office needed enlarging, city leaders were forced to decommission their other engineering marvel.

Twice as Ice

If you try to belly up to Crested Butte's Ice Bar in July, all I can say is, "Good luck." At that time of year, the fifteen-stool outdoor bar that sells specialty martinis is most likely watering wildflowers at the base of Twister Lift.

Like Brigadoon, the Scottish village that appears only one day every century, the Ice Bar is invisible much of the year—but that can happen when you're made entirely of frozen water. The Ice Bar is constructed each winter (usually by Thanksgiving) from giant ice-filled trash cans, drenched with water and frozen into place. Like African violets, the bar must be watered nearly every day to hold its shape.

The waitresses and bartenders at the Ice Bar, who have been known to wear fur bikinis (underneath their mink coats, of course), serve martinis, wine, and other libations. Inside the adjoining Ice Bar restaurant (that thankfully doesn't melt in the summer), skiers can sit down to an on-mountain gourmet meal complete with white tablecloths.

At the Ice Bar's inauguration, the all-female staff wore thrift-store furs.
Tom Stillo/Crested Butte Mountain Resort

The Ice Bar is near the base of Twister Lift, and several evenings during ski season, guests can ride the Red Lady Express Lift to the Ice Bar for the Last Tracks Dinner, which features such delicacies as mesquite-smoked rainbow trout, blue corn chiles rellenos, and roasted pepper couscous. After dinner, a procession on snowshoes, skis, or snowboard is led back down the mountain by torchlight. Call (800) 544-8448 for more information.

Telluride

Telluride is living *proof that the theory of evolution exists.*

Just like the beaks of Darwin's finches, separated on the far-flung Galapagos Islands, morphed into odd sizes and shapes, the town of Telluride, separated from the rest of the world in a box canyon, has morphed into an odd haven for the quirky, artistic, and rare. "To hell with the rest of the world" could well be the town mantra. That's why Telluride is the only mountain town besides Crested Butte to warrant it's own chapter.

Not that the rest of the world doesn't manage to find its way to this tiny town sitting smack dab at the finale of a two-lane, dead-end road. The skiing alone mandates it as a destination for bicoastal glitterati to come and be rich together. Throw in the scenery (a fabulous glacial valley, waterfalls, and the white incisors of the San Juan Mountains) and what choice did Oprah, Tom Cruise, and Oliver Stone have but to buy property and force locals to nickname it Telluwood.

But no matter who comes, who stays, who nicknames it what, Telluride is going to be Telluride, true to its own evolution from a nine-teenth-century mining town to one of the most unique places on the planet.

The closest stoplight is 65 miles away. Strip malls? Neon? Drive-ins? What's that? The whole town is a designated National Historic District and has been for over forty years. Woe be it to any chain that tries to breach this hallowed place.

Is it any wonder that locals have names like Art Goodtimes (he's a county commissioner, an organic potato farmer, and the owner of a beat-up pickup painted red with white spots to advertise the town's annual Mushroom Festival), Captain Jack (he's a sixty-something ski bum with a white long beard), and Big Bird Gesus, who wears diamonds in his teeth, an eagle's head under his beret, and came up with a plan to build a glass pyramid-cum-overpass for the deer to cross the canyons safely. So far, that plan is still just a plan.

Call me old-fashioned, but there's something about a town that has its own commercial-free radio station (it's not unheard of to hear five and a half straight hours of Bob Dylan), its own marching band (being able to play an instrument is not a prerequisite), and its own quirky economy of sharing, scrounging, and bartering that makes me want to laugh out loud, that makes me want to kick those cookie-cutter towns with all their Wal-Marts and McDonald's right in their homogenized Chicken McNuggets.

In fact, my highest hope for this book is that you'll buy lots and lots of copies, and then I can afford to move to Telluride.

★ ★

Of Being and Nothingness

Telluride has rightly earned its moniker as the Festival City. Every weekend in the spring, summer, and fall, you can pretty much bet that some festival or another is going to be held. There's the Mushroom Festival, the Bluegrass Festival, the Film Festival, the Beer and Blues Festival . . . The list goes on. And on.

In 1991 local Dennis Wrestler, who was tired of all these high-profile festivals that ballooned the town's meager population of 2,000 to 10,000 or more, wrote a tongue-in-cheek letter to the city manager requesting a "Nothing Festival."

He was taken seriously, and, quicker than he could yawn, the Nothing Festival was added to the docket. It has been held every summer since. The festival's motto, of course, is "Leave Me Alone"; instead of a security staff, there's an "insecurity staff"; and since wristbands are not needed, guests are invited to find a tiny piece of string and tie it around their wrist. Events include:

1. Sunrises and sunsets as normal
2. Gravity continuing to be in effect
3. The laws of physics on display

You can even print out your own VIP pass at the Nothing Festival's Web site (see below) that entitles you to unlimited access to all events, front-row seats, backstage passes, national security briefing, and rides with the Blue Angels precision team. Of course, the pass is contingent on actually having any events, seats, stages, or Blue Angels.

To buy a T-shirt (they're $15 if you have a sense of humor, $20 if you don't), contact the Telluride Nothing Festival at P.O. Box 10, Placerville, CO 81430; or visit the Web site at www.telluridenothing festival.com. In closing, the organizers of this festival would like to say, "Don't call, don't buy tickets, and don't register." And last but not least, "Thank you for not participating."

Free Furs for Everyone

Practically every fourth window of Telluride's century-old storefronts has posters of multimillion-dollar real estate listings.

Still, you can't quibble with the prices at Telluride's Free Box. Everything at the do-it-yourself Salvation Army on Pine Street goes for free, nada, zilch. Locals drop off old (and sometimes new) items such as skis, sweaters, TVs, and, according to rumor, keys to used cars.

The price is right at Telluride's infamous Free Box.
Jerry Greene/Baked in Telluride

★ ★

Everybody in town has a story about some amazing find they snagged at the Free Box, from bottles of Scotch to camel hair coats to Prada handbags. Once in the mid-1980s, when a fur store tried to make it in Telluride, animal rights protesters (or at least they were the main suspects) broke in, snagged the minks, and left five of the $20,000 coats in the Free Box for the taking.

Though the Free Box started as a real box, set out in front of a health food store in 1976, it has grown into a much tidier set of wooden bins that are cleared out at least once a week. A Free Box mosaic is embedded into the nearby wall, and if you browse at Between the Covers, a local bookshop, you'll find a whole book written about Free Box fashion.

The Free Box is located on Pine Street right off Colorado Avenue.

Way Up, Up, and Away

The Telluride Airport, sitting at 9,078 feet at the top of Deep Creek Mesa, is the highest commercial airport in North America. It's also the only airport in the world that partly supports itself with a rock quarry.

If you're a pilot, there are three things you need to know about the Telluride Airport:

1. The airport is closed after sunset, partly because noise regulations are in effect, but also because the Federal Aviation Administration didn't think night flights were particularly prudent, as the airport is virtually surrounded by 14,000-foot obstacles.
2. The runways are short enough that jumbo jets should reroute to Montrose, even if it is a seventy-minute drive on winding, two-lane highways.
3. The views are breathtaking. Try hard not to notice.

The Telluride Airport, only seven minutes from downtown Telluride, can be reached by US Airways, Frontier, and Great Lakes Air. The address (maybe you should take this as an omen) is 1500 Last Dollar Road; phone (970) 728-5051.

La Cage aux Ski

Skiers disagree on the best clothes for the slopes. Some wouldn't be caught dead without a Lycra racing suit. Others swear by Bogner or $3,000 Spyder I-Pod jackets. In Telluride, however, the best ski outfit might be a blond wig, falsies, and a hula skirt—at least if you plan to enter the Robert Presley Memorial In-Drag Race, an annual event started in 1995 along with the Telluride AIDS Benefit.

This tongue-in-cheek, on-mountain costume race pits men as women against women as men against all other gender interpretations. How fast you ski is beside the point. Prizes go for how flamboyantly you can pull off that Marilyn Monroe imitation or that Boy George smirk.

The race started when friends of Robert Presley, a larger-than-life Telluride costume designer, discovered he was coping with AIDS sans health insurance. Pal Kandee DeGraw, an actor with the Telluride Repertory Theater, decided to chip in with Presley's mounting medical bills. She organized a fashion show (it amounted to actors from the Rep dressing in garbage bags and clothes plucked from the Free Box) and the "In-Drag" ski race, both events that have since grown to monumental proportions. The Telluride AIDS Benefit (TAB) is the largest single contributor to the Western Colorado AIDS Project (Presley wouldn't hear of it benefiting him alone), which services hundreds of clients in twenty-two counties and donates more than $10,000 a year to Manzini, Swaziland, Telluride's sister city.

Although Presley succumbed to AIDS in August 1997, his outrageous costumes live on in the memories of anyone lucky enough to have attended the early fashion shows. His backless vinyl smocks, modeled by Telluride's most cheeky denizens, reflected not only his long, humiliating, butt-exposed waits in exam offices, but also his over-the-top vivacious personality. Models, all Telluride locals, were picked for their willingness to strut the runways in PVC tubing, skirts made of Hershey's Kisses, or just plain paint.

Today the show, just as funky, is stocked with the fashions of dozens of Donna Karan wannabes from all over the country who jump at

★ ★

the chance to participate in one of the most unique runway shows in the world.

For more information about this three-ring circus, check out the TAB Web site at www.aidsbenefit.org, or call (970) 728-0869.

We Need a Little Thanksgiving, Right This Very Minute

For most of us, Thanksgiving prayers go something like this: "Thank God that's over with." But in Telluride, Thanksgiving dinners complete with roasted turkey and all the trimmings are served each and every Thursday.

Move Over, Paris

Paris, as everyone knows, is called the "City of Lights." But long before Paris got electricity or was lit by anything but candles, tiny Telluride, Colorado, had full running electricity and was the first town on the planet to have electric street lamps.

And it was all thanks to an archenemy of Thomas Alva Edison. Nikola Tesla, who developed the world's first alternating current (AC) power plant in the mountains above Telluride, didn't start out feuding with the more famous inventor. In fact, Edison, recognizing Tesla's genius, promised him $50,000 if he would solve a problem he was having with an electrical dynamo. When Tesla fixed the problem, the competitive Edison insisted he had been joking and refused to pay. He also waged a vicious campaign to discredit his associate's inventions that harnessed alternating current.

For years, Edison and Tesla represented two sides of what was known as the AC/DC Current Wars. Edison insisted direct current (DC) was the way to go, even going so far as to introduce legislation to

Jerry Greene, who moved to Telluride some thirty years ago to help establish KOTO, the noncommercial radio station, can't remember exactly when he started offering weekly turkey dinners complete with mashed potatoes, French-cut green beans, cranberry sauce with wildflower honey, and stuffing, but he knows it's been at least fifteen years. For the first thirteen or so, the lavish holiday meals were served every Thursday except Thanksgiving. But then in 2003, his employees at the popular bakery called Baked in Telluride said they didn't mind doing it on the real-deal day as well.

Besides being a turkey aficionado, Greene relishes making New York–style bagels, the kind New Yorkers smugly believe they can

limit power transmission to 800 volts. Tesla campaigned for alternating current. Edison tried vainly to frighten the public about the dangers of AC by electrocuting cats and dogs. Tesla countered by passing thousands of volts through his own body.

In 1891 Tesla, who was working with George Westinghouse on the alternating current side, jumped at a Telluride mine owner's offer to fund the first commercial AC power plant, even if it was 11,000 feet up the side of a mountain. Entrepreneur L. L. Nunn, who made his initial Telluride money by building the town's first bathtub, recognized that if he was going to make his Gold King mine profitable, he needed to find a better way to distribute power. He took a train to New York and offered Tesla and Westinghouse $100,000 and the manpower to give the new technology its first test.

Although the Gold King mine never became profitable, Nunn's newly formed Telluride Power Company went on to build twelve power plants, all patterned after Telluride's first commercial high-voltage transmission of alternating current.

★ ★

Thanksgiving fifty-two weeks a year.
Jerry Greene/Baked in Telluride

get only in Manhattan. Even though he's originally from New Jersey, Greene has been known to run ads proclaiming his bagels' superiority in the venerable *New York Times.* Known locally as B-I-T, Greene's bakery makes everything from donuts to bagels, bialys to Danishes, muffins to pizza dough, all hand-tossed from scratch.

B-I-T is located in a red corrugated-steel warehouse built in 1892 at 127 South Fir Street. The phone number is (970) 728-4775.

Before Beer Commercials

Who can really dispute that the most Oscar-worthy commercials on TV revolve around beer, particularly "lite" beer? But before Super Bowls and wacky beer ads, beer makers relied on other methods to market their suds. Labels, which suck in thirsty beer guzzlers by the six-pack, played a significant role. That's why Coors went straight to Wilson Peak near Telluride for its model of "Pure Rocky Mountain spring water."

For years, 14,017-foot Wilson Peak has been the spokesmountain for Coors beer, the magnificent backdrop on every label. Like Mount Wilson, its 14-footer cousin to the left, Wilson Peak was named after A. D. Wilson, who surveyed the Rocky Mountains with the Hayden Survey of 1877.

Although you can't exactly miss a 14,000-foot mountain, especially when you've seen it a thousand times on the front of a beer can, just keep your eyes peeled on the west side of CO 145. It's about 11 miles from town as the crow flies.

Contact the USFS Norwood Ranger District at (970) 327-4261 for information on access to Wilson Peak.

World's Oldest Profession Gets Culture

Back when Telluride was a rowdy, gun-slinging mining town, Popcorn Alley was the place to be if you were a miner hankering for female companionship. A whole row of "female boardinghouses" sprung up on Pacific Street: the Senate, the Silver Belle, the Cribs, and the Madam's Stone, to name just a few of the brothels that flourished from the 1880s to 1930s.

In 1991 the Silver Belle, which had also served as a soda parlor (wink-wink) during Prohibition, was restored to its resplendent glory and reopened as the Ah Haa School for the Arts, an institution whose stated mission is as follows: "Creativity in all its fantastical forms is needed to make the world a better place."

Classes are offered year-round in everything from photography to silver making to Japanese box making. The American Academy of Bookbinding, an internationally known school for old-time leather bookbinding, operates from Ah Haa, as does the Talking Gourd poetry series that invites poets, storytellers, singers, actors, and writers of any ilk to share their words, creations, and performances in regular open-mike nights.

Ah Haa is located at 135 South Spruce Street. For more information, call (970) 728-3886, or visit their Web site at www.ahhaa.org.

★ ★

Good Mormon Gone Bad

Every day for a month, twenty-three-year-old Butch Cassidy, who had driven some cattle to Telluride from his home in Utah, walked into the San Miguel Valley Bank to make a small deposit. He always wore a suit, always smiled politely, and always, as soon as he walked out the door, shot his guns into the air, hooted and hollered, and made a big commotion. After a while, people got used to it: Oh, that's just that crazy Mormon kid making his daily rounds.

Except on June 24, 1889, when Butch Cassidy came out shooting and hollering, with bank officials at his heels, it was not like any other day. The well-dressed Mormon had just robbed the bank of $22,000, every last red cent.

It's a charming story, and you'll inevitably hear it if you stick around Telluride long enough. There's just one problem: It's not exactly true.

Butch Cassidy *did* rob the San Miguel Valley Bank. And it was the first in a long string of bank robberies that turned the young Mormon into a legend. But like all legends, it soon took on a life of its own.

In fact, remember that movie *Butch Cassidy and the Sundance Kid,* when Butch (played by Paul Newman) and Sundance (played by Robert Redford) were gunned down in the end by Bolivian militia? Well, in 1969, after the movie became a smash hit, reporters began nosing around Cassidy's childhood home in Circleville, Utah. Lula Parker Betenson, Butch's youngest sister, who was eighty-six at the time, informed a reporter that her notorious brother had not died in South America in 1909 as was widely believed. In fact, she said he came to pay a visit in 1925 and didn't kick the bucket until 1937 after a long career in Spokane, Washington, as a trapper and prospector.

Sure enough, scholars have found evidence that in all likelihood Butch Cassidy did fake his death in San Vicente, Bolivia, sailed to Europe, got a facelift, moved back to America, and became an entrepreneur in Washington.

The San Miguel Valley Bank is no longer in business, but there's a plaque where it used to sit, marking it as the first in a long, illustrious career, and the safe Butch heisted is still around at Sunglass HQ at 201 West Colorado Avenue.

If I Should Die Before I Wake

Hotels are always coming up with gimmicks to attract more guests. Stay for five nights, get the sixth night free. Book a week, score tickets to Disneyland. Or Sea World. Or . . . well, you know the shtick.

The New Sheridan in Telluride, a fabulous historic hotel built in 1895 that probably doesn't need any gimmicks, offers the most

The gathering spot for Telluride's glitterati.
New Sheridan

★ ★

unusual incentive of all. Their promise? If you should die while staying at the New Sheridan, they'll pick up the cost of your funeral.

I should probably explain. The original Sheridan Hotel, built four years before the current brick one, was a three-story wooden structure. In 1894, just three years after its illustrious grand opening, it was leveled to the ground by a raging fire, a fact that, as you can imagine, made guests of the new hotel a tad bit antsy.

When the owners erected the New Sheridan, a fireproof brick hotel next to the charred lot, they decided to reassure customers by making the unique offer. Far as I know, the offer still stands.

Not that the historic jewel needs many incentives. Its first-floor saloon, complete with a cherrywood bar from Austria, is one of the hottest spots in town; its restaurant, the Continental Room, has sixteen velvet-curtained booths; and guests who stay in one of the thirty-two Victorian-period rooms get their choice of a half-dozen pillow styles. No wonder presidential candidate William Jennings Bryan chose to deliver his "Cross of Gold" speech on a platform right outside the front door.

The New Sheridan is located at 231 West Colorado Avenue and can be reached at (970) 728-4351 or (800) 200-1891; the Web site is www.newsheridan.com.

When the Going Gets Tough, the Tough Get Goosey

During the Depression when the Rio Grande Southern was about to go down the tubes, the enterprising railroad decided to give it one last college try. Since they could no longer afford to run steam locomotives on their 162 miles of narrow-gauge track, they developed a homemade, half-baked, gas-powered contraption that ran at a fraction of the cost. Their Rube Goldberg–inspired engineers took an old Buick, painted it silver, and dubbed it the Galloping Goose since it waddled as it traversed the tracks and had a squawking air horn.

The goose was so successful (not to mention all the attention it received) that the $828 construction costs were recouped in no time. Needless to say, the company quickly embarked on an even bigger

Horseplay

Local cowboy/hippie Roudy Roudebush gave up drinking years ago, but that doesn't stop him from riding his mare, Golly-G, through the swinging doors of Telluride's saloons. He runs Telluride Horseback Adventures when he's not skiing (he gets a free ski pass for his highfalutin antics around town).

"I took precautions early in life to keep myself unemployable, leaving myself free to ski and ride horses," Roudy quips.

He arrived in Telluride in the summer of 1970, three years before the skiing opened, and back then, he says, "We drank in order to reach a higher level of consciousness, and as there were no jobs, we didn't have to feel guilty."

By 1973 he opened Telluride Unstable, which, of course, must have set him on the path to open his stable business out on Last Dollar Road.

goose made from a Pierce-Arrow limousine. Eventually, they even modified Wayne buses with surplus army GM engines under the hoods.

Between 1931 and 1936 seven galloping geese were thrown together, breathing two more decades of life into the railroad that carried mail, freight, and eventually passengers to the remote mining communities in the San Juan Mountains. These innovative rattletraps kept the Rio Grande Southern afloat long enough to haul uranium for the Manhattan Project and carry tourists, who called years in advance to get a reservation on the scenic route.

The tourists didn't come until later, though, when the U.S. Postal Service finally pulled the mail contract. Ever innovative, the Rio Grande Southern cut window slots in the sides of the freight boxes and installed a concession counter to sell box lunches. I've heard that during the late 1940s, the Galloping Goose was even more popular

★ ★

than the Grand Canyon. But despite its brave and creative initiative, the Rio Grande Southern finally embraced a fate a half century in the making and shut down in 1952.

Goose #4 is located in front of the San Miguel County Courthouse, and Telluride's free bus service (a moot point since everything is within walking distance anyway) is called the Galloping Goose. Like its name-sake, Galloping Goose #101 is innovative enough to run on renewable, nontoxic, biodegradable, vegetable oil–based biodiesel fuel.

All the World's a DJ

One out of every ten residents of Telluride is a licensed, FCC-registered DJ. That's because Telluride has one of the nation's only commercial-free, non-underwritten listener-supported radio stations. It's called KOTO, its motto is "Radio Almost Like the Professionals," and it's the town's de facto soundtrack, whether you're in Honga's Lotus Petal, a great Asian restaurant on Colorado Avenue; at the Jag-ged Edge, an outdoor clothing company launched nationally from Telluride; or picking up a bottle of BIOTA at Clark's Market. Locals who are fly fishermen, Rastafarian drummers, or ski patrol by day host such shows as Cows with Guns Dharma Bum, Jamaican Me Crazy (which not only has island music, but "songs you love to hate" and kids' songs), and The G-Spot, which advertises itself as "great music to take apart a mountain bike to."

Indeed, the "almost like professionals" motto sells itself short. The popular radio station has a 3,000-watt tower, three call letters, and can be heard all over the world by anyone with streaming Web access. KOTO, which has almost as many fun, wacky fund-raisers (name that tune, for example, or lip-sync contests with locals singing "I'm Too Sexy" dressed as Tibetan monks) as they do DJs, closes down the main drag every year in April for an end-of-the-ski-season jubilee and a free street dance. Notables such as Jackson Browne (yes, that Jackson Browne) have come to town to perform for the big KOTO Doo Dah.

KOTO has been around since 1975 and is really proud of the fact that it provides news, information, and entertainment that members (as opposed to commercial or corporate interests) define. For example, if you lose your dog Max, just call the station, and hosts will ask on air if anyone has seen him. Anybody who's anybody in Telluride is either a KOTO DJ, a KOTO listener, or at least a regular walk-in to the KOTO studio that has always been located in the heart of downtown.

All are welcome to hang out at the KOTO studio that's situated in the house behind the Miner's Union at 207 North Pine Street.

Alice in Mushroomland

You know those cute little red mushrooms with the white spots? Well, don't even think about eating one. It'll send you on a psychedelic journey that only Timothy Leary knew about. And that's just one

Art Goodtimes's truck doesn't always sport a mushroom, but it's painted red with polka dots 24-7-365.
Iris Willow

of the juicy tidbits you'll pick up at the world-famous Telluride Mushroom Festival.

Other tidbits—porcini, chanterelle, lobster, and matsutake, to name a few of the 400 types of identifiable mushrooms—are gourmet, and you'll find them on daily mushroom-hunting forays. And, yes, you are highly encouraged to eat as many of those as you can possibly stuff into your craw during Telluride's annual three-day 'shroom fest. Perhaps the highlight of this part zany, part serious event (alternative medical guru Andrew Weil has been known to lead workshops) is the mushroom parade that features dogs dressed as mushrooms, city commissioners posing as mushrooms, and tattooed mushrooms turning cartwheels. There are also mushroom cook-offs, mushroom poetry competitions, and mushroom movies.

The Mushroom Festival's poet laureate, Art Goodtimes, who also happens to be a county commissioner and organic potato farmer, drives a red truck with white spots to symbolize the colorful but trip-invoking mushroom.

For information about this festival honoring fungus, visit www .shroomfestival.com.

Hope He Doesn't Walk in His Sleep

In case you're counting, there are a grand total of four Bridal Veil Falls in Colorado alone. The popular waterfall name also shows up in New Zealand, Australia, Canada, Zimbabwe, and most of the other U.S. states, including one of the Niagara Falls. But the Bridal Veil Falls in Telluride stands above for two main reasons. First of all, at 365 feet, it's the highest waterfall in Colorado. And second, it's the only Bridal Veil Falls with a man-made structure teetering on top.

Built as a power plant for the Smuggler-Union Mine, which, at one time, had a 2-mile vein of silver, the wooden structure is now a single-family home, although I heard the owner's wife divorced him after tiring of the 1.8-mile hike from the nearest grocery store. "That 1.8 miles wouldn't be so bad," she probably said, "but the 1,200-foot ascent, forget it."

Captain Jack Is Already High Tonight?

If you look up *ski bum* in the dictionary, you'll likely see a picture of Captain Jack Carey. At sixty-something, this balding Telluride ski bum who looks like a member of ZZ Top (he hasn't cut his white beard since 1991, and last time anybody measured, it was at least 3 feet long) has perfected the art of scratching out a living doing what he loves most—skiing. Oh sure, his multipage résumé also includes dish washing, table waiting, bar tending, and gas pumping, but his most notorious accomplishment is the fact that he's spent the last three decades logging at least 120 ski days a winter.

Captain Jack started life the normal way, attending college, joining the air force, and teaching high school history in New Hampshire. But after a fateful vacation to Colorado in 1972, he rearranged his priorities, mailing in his teaching resignation just before the fall term.

He likes to say that if there were such a thing as a doctorate in ski bumming, he'd have earned it. But unlike some ski bums, who never marry or own real estate, Captain Jack has a wife and a 1,800-square-foot home only eight minutes from the nearest lift. Although his yearly income is lower than what some Telluride transplants spend yearly on liposuction, he pays taxes, is fully insured, and has absolutely no debt. "For me the American dream hasn't been about high-paying jobs or expensive possessions—it's been about living an adventurous life."

If you ski Telluride, you can't miss Captain Jack, who also holds a number of altitude and endurance records as a hang glider (after all, you have to do something in the summer). He's the guy with the long beard and the big smile.

To get there, just follow the switchbacks (there's a sign for Bridal Veil Falls) at the east end of Colorado Avenue, Telluride's main drag.

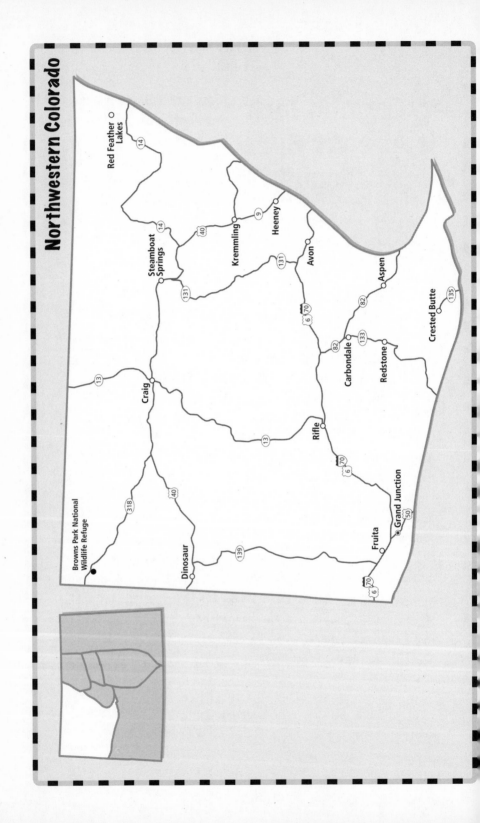

Northwestern Colorado

8

Northwestern Colorado

As much as I'd like to, I just can't rein in the superlatives when talking about northwestern Colorado. There are just too many world's largests and world's firsts in this part of the state to remain humble.

For starters, there's the world's largest unicycle in Grand Junction and the world's largest beaver dam outside Rifle. Then there's the world's largest headless chicken festival in Fruita and the world's largest flattop mountain in Grand Mesa.

And if that weren't enough, the world's first taxi to have strobes, disco lights, a telescope, and a dry-ice machine was inaugurated in Aspen, and the world's first bridge to be named Bob was built in Aspen.

So if you notice a glaring lack of modesty, forgive me.

★ ★

On the Flipside
Aspen

Depending on who you talk to, the one-finger salute (also known in some circles as "flipping the bird") painted on the roof of the house north of Aspen is a message either to the Aspen/Pitkin County Airport or to the owner's ex-wife. Those in the airport camp say the owner of the house was asked by muckety-mucks to repaint the once-shiny roof because it was "blinding airplanes" coming in to Sardy Field, and this was his alleged response.

Those in the ex-wife league claim the finger is a tribute to the guy's bitter divorce. Story has it that he wanted to make sure the ex saw it every time she flew in and out of the airport with her new, rich hubby. By now, he's probably forgiven her since the tribute first went up twenty years ago. Of course, you never know. The colorful bird is periodically updated and edited with fresh paint.

To see the infamous "one-fingered peace sign" that for a while was rumored to belong to Hunter S. Thompson (it didn't—he lived on the other side of town), take CO 82 north out of Aspen. Or keep your eyes open when flying into Sardy Field.

Beam Me Up, Taxi
Aspen

Back in 1984, when ski bum Jon Barnes landed a killer deal on a 1978 Checker cab, he decided to leave the restaurant business behind. He'd had enough of bussing tables and tending bar, and besides, he'd always wanted to be his own boss. Heck, with his own taxi, he could ski during the day and ferry Aspen guests at night.

At first, Barnes was happy with the simple cab. So what if it had 75,000 miles on it? Oh, he added a police scanner, an awesome sound system, and a couple other perks, but that was mostly for his own enjoyment.

But in 1990 he had a stroke of genius that has turned him and his taxi into an international phenomenon. He decided to add strobes, a

If you are an insurance adjuster, this photo is not for you.
Jon Barnes

fog machine, disco lights, a dry-ice machine, stage lights, neon, and a multidisk CD/DVD system. And if that doesn't entertain his passengers, he has a telescope (for spotting alien invasions) and digital drums and a keyboard on which they can produce their own music. He has enough wattage in his cab to brown out your average Kansas village.

Barnes, realizing he was on to a good thing, renamed his yellow cab the Ultimate Taxi and taught himself to do magic tricks (while stopped at a stoplight, of course) and play the sax. Driving with his elbows, he croons Pink Floyd and other classic rock while a laser light show, enhanced by diffraction glasses and fog, wows his guests. He even downloads photos of his passengers (Jerry Seinfeld, Clint Eastwood,

★ ★

Pierce Brosnan, and Lee Iacocca, to name a few) onto the Internet.

The one essential of being an Ultimate Taxi driver is, says Barnes, "you have to have an insurance company that has never actually seen inside your car."

To catch a ride in the five-seat rolling theater, contact Barnes at (970) 927-9239. You can check out his passengers' photos at www .ultimatetaxi.com.

A Bridge Named Bob

Avon

In 1991 Avon, a town that tends to get lost between flashy Vail and Beaver Creek, made international headlines when it named its new bridge across the Eagle River "Bob."

Yes, you read that right. A bridge named Bob.

In a name-that-bridge contest that garnered eighty-four entries, the good, old-fashioned name of "Bob" beat out finalists "Avon Crossing" and "Del Mayne Crossing" in a 4–2 vote by the town council.

The name created such a stir that for a while Avon threw an annual Bobfest for guys named Bob. Over the years, the festival attracted as many as 10,000 Bobs, Wannabobs, Married to Bobs, Know a Bobs, and I Wish I Was a Bobs. Those who go by "Robert" were not allowed to participate. Among the attractions at the now-deceased Bobfest were Bob-R-Shop Quartets, a Bob-B-Que, and Bob, Bob Bobbing Along, a white-water raft trip to Bob. There were also competitive events like lawn mower racing and 50-yard dashes to the refrigerator. The only downside to having a famous bridge is that your name can get diluted. To lots of folks, Avon is not Avon. It's Bobtown.

Bob, the four-lane span that crosses the Eagle River, connects I-70 with US 6.

Forget Pirate Maps
Browns Park National Wildlife Refuge

I wish I could draw you a map that would lead right to the bank-robbin' booty that Butch Cassidy and his Wild Bunch left behind in Moffat County, but that would spoil all the fun.

A good place to start looking, of course, is Browns Park National Wildlife Refuge. This isolated 50-mile valley that lies along the Green River is hours of two-lane highway from the nearest ski resort, which could be why the loot that Butch and his gang stashed there has never been recovered.

The Wild Bunch obviously didn't know their hideout would some-day be an official wildlife refuge. They just called it Browns Hole. They liked the fact that officers of the law didn't frequent the place and that those who came in chase lost their quarry almost immediately. They also liked to visit the Basset Ranch run by matriarch Elizabeth Basset—and her two comely daughters, Ann and Josie—who besides being a lover of Butch, was married five times and accused of cattle rustling herself when she was sixty-two.

Butch and his boys weren't the first ruffians to frequent the remote valley, far from the long arm of the law. Juan Jose Herrera, a native of New Mexico, came to Browns Hole in 1870 with the mission of start-ing his own cattle business—with other ranchers' cattle.

Even today, brochures for the wildlife refuge warn people think-ing of coming to see the migratory fowl that they'll be driving on gravel roads, situated a good 50 miles from the nearest town, and even those two towns, Maybell and Dutch John (which is in Utah), offer minimal services. Finding a hotel is nearly as impossible as find-ing Butch's treasure. But if you do find the booty, my commission is a mere 15 percent.

For more information about Browns Park National Wildlife Refuge, write 1318 Highway 318, Maybell, CO 81640; or call (970) 365-3613; www.fws.gov/brownspark.

★ ★

A Weed by Any Other Name
Carbondale

The curse of most home owners has won a special place in the hearts of Carbondale residents. Yes, the dandelion, the very same flower that most of us eschew as a pesky weed, is a celebrated guest of honor in this town just 30 miles from Aspen. A Carbondale city ordinance prohibits using pesticides on dandelions, and locals use them to make food, beer, and medicine. If you stop by city hall, they'll gladly give you some dandelion recipes, including one using the roots that makes a passable substitute for coffee. They even have a festival every year honoring the official town flower. It's called Dandelion Day, of course, and its motto is "If you can't beat it, eat it."

Doc Phillips, a chiropractor in Carbondale who started the festival,

Hail, dandelion!
Carbondale Chamber of Commerce

says this: "Turns out that dandelions are not weeds, but vegetables. In fact, they're among the most nutritious vegetables on the planet. Kale and spinach come close, but ask any ethnobotanist, dandelions have them all beat."

Carbondale's mission to raise the world's dandelion conscious-ness happened inadvertently when the city, growing too fast for its own good, was forced to divert park pesticide funds to the building of roads and sewer systems. One day, Doc and others realized that Sopris Park was filled with 100 percent nonpesticidal organic dandeli-ons, which they quickly plucked to make food, beer, and wine.

For a while, community activist Ed Eaton even used dandelions as a staple in the dishes he sold at his Solar Cafe, a short-lived street cafe with all entrees cooked in his homemade solar oven. Eaton made dan-delion lasagne and dandelion tamales, to name a couple delicacies.

Admittedly, there are still a few folks in Carbondale who believe the only good dandelion is a dead dandelion. But they usually come out anyway for Dandelion Day, which includes dandelion cook-offs, dandelion wine tastings, dandelion poetry competitions, dandelion face painting, and one heck of a costume parade called "The Proces-sion of the Species."

For more information about Carbondale's obsession with the ubiq-uitous weed, contact the chamber of commerce at (970) 963-1890.

My Daughter, the Car
Craig

Most city parks have a slide, a couple swings, and a bandstand on which the town orchestra attempts to play John Philip Sousa. The city park in Craig, Colorado, has tennis courts, a wave pool, and a luxury railroad car that's listed on the National Register of Historic Places. If you call (970) 824-5689, you can even score your own personal tour of the Marcia, as the customized railroad car is called.

Named after railroad magnate David Moffat's only daughter, the

★ ★

Marcia was Moffat's personal business car. There are stained-glass windows, an all-wood interior custom-built from African mahogany, and beds for twelve. The personalized silver ice bucket alone recently sold for $2,500.

The Marcia was built in 1906 while David Moffat was busy constructing the Denver Northwestern & Pacific Railroad. Starting in Denver, the railroad that Moffat wanted to take all the way to Salt Lake made it as far as Craig. Unfortunately, Moffat and his investors ran short of cash. Their railroad languished in Craig until 1947, when it was reorganized and merged with the Denver & Rio Grande Western Railroad. The fancy car was given to Craig in 1953.

Wonder what the rich folks are doing tonight.
Max Sims/Craig Chamber of Commerce

✶ ✶

The Marcia is located at 360 East Victory Way in Craig in Moffat County, a county that's roughly the same size as the entire state of Connecticut.

A Postman's Worst Nightmare

Dinosaur

Neither rain, nor sleet, nor the changing of Elm Street to Triceratops Terrace will keep mail carriers from making their appointed rounds.

Located a mere 3 miles from the Utah border, the small town of Dinosaur used to have a different name. Until 1966 this burg of 345 was known as Artesia. But then town leaders, being the capitalists town leaders tend to be, decided to latch on to the popularity of nearby Dinosaur National Monument. By a near unanimous vote, they decided to change the moniker listed on the WELCOME TO . . . sign. And if that wasn't challenging enough for local mail carriers, they then proceeded to change the names of all the streets—there's Brontosaurus Boulevard, for example. Stegosaurus Freeway, Diplodicus Drive, and Brachiosaurus Bypass are a few others you'll find in Colorado's westernmost town. And even though the town's population could practically fit in five phone booths, its Loaf N' Jug convenience store sells the second most lottery tickets in all of Colorado, thanks, we assume, to Mormons from Utah.

Colorado Tourism staffs a visitor center at 101 Stegosaurus Freeway; (970) 374-2205.

Look Ma, No Head

Fruita

Fruita has the unique distinction of hosting the world's largest headless chicken festival. Of course, the annual event is probably the world's only headless chicken festival. After all, it's not just any town that can claim a celebrity who survived eighteen months without a noggin.

★ ★

It all started September 10, 1945, when Clara Olsen's mother was coming for a visit. In preparation, Clara sent her husband, Lloyd, out to butcher one of their prize Wyandotte roosters. Being the good husband (plus it never hurts to score brownie points with the mother-in-law), Lloyd plucked up a rooster, grabbed the ax, and unceremoniously whacked off its head. Like most recently dispatched poultry, it flapped around for a while, but instead of eventually keeling over, it continued to breathe, right through its severed windpipe. Lloyd figured any chicken with that strong of a will deserved to live, mother-in-law be damned.

He named the hapless chicken Mike and figured out a way to feed it by mixing grain with water and dispensing it with an eyedropper. After a week and a weight gain of nearly half a pound, Lloyd packed up Mike in his farm truck and drove the 250 miles to the University of Utah for answers. The skeptical scientists finally determined that the ax blade had missed the jugular and a fast-acting clot saved Mike from bleeding to death. His head was in a jar, but the brainstem and one ear that was left were enough to preserve his reflexes.

In the eighteen months that followed, Mike lived as "The Headless Wonder Chicken" and grew from a mere 2½ pounds to nearly 8 pounds. Mike's excellent health made it difficult for animal rights activists to garner much of a following. Instead, Miracle Mike took on a manager and, with the Olsens in tow, set out on a national tour. Curious sideshow patrons in New York, Atlantic City, Los Angeles, and San Diego lined up to pay 25 cents to see the chicken that was valued at $10,000 and insured for the same. He eventually earned recognition in *Life* and *Time* magazines and won a well-deserved Guinness World Record.

Today, the good citizens of Fruita honor their most famous native son with his own personal Web site (see below), a larger-than-life-size statue made of horseshoes and hand tools, and the two-day festival that includes bands, chicken recipe competitions, and a race called

"Run Like a Headless Chicken." But as city leaders are quick to point out, "We're celebrating Mike's impressive will to live, not the nature of his handicap."

Fruita is on I-70 about 10 miles west of Grand Junction. The festival is held the third weekend in May. For more information, see Mike's Web site at www.miketheheadlesschicken.org.

As You Bike It
Grand Junction

In 1976 a Grand Junction resident named Jim Petty claimed the record for riding the world's tallest unicycle. His 30-foot unicycle, according to Dave Bailey, the curator of the Museum of Western Colorado, is gathering dust somewhere in the museum's storage.

For a while it was on display, right there next to the dinosaur exhibits, but eventually the powers-that-oversee-these-things decided that exhibits like Alferd Packer's 1862 Colt Police Model pistol and his journal, the one that eventually proved his innocence, were more interesting to museum patrons. Even in the History of Pictures Project, a venture the museum undertook with the Mesa County Historical Society, the transportation segment of the 1970s chose to feature the first hot-air balloon rally in 1978 rather than the big unicycle two years earlier.

Oh well! That's what Petty gets for packing up and leaving the area. In fact, if you call the Jim Petty that lives in Grand Junction now, he'll tell you he knows nothing about the giant unicycle. But he can sure tell you about a giant high chair (as big as a house, he claims) that sat downtown for several years until the powers-that-oversee-these-things decided to take it down.

The Museum of Western Colorado is located at 462 Ute Avenue in Grand Junction; (970) 242-0971; www.museumofwesternco.com.

★ ★

Wilma!!!!

Grand Junction

Before my trip to Grand Junction, my knowledge of dinosaurs was limited to the Flintstones. And while I'm not sure if Dino was a brontosaurus, a stegosaurus, or a tyrannosaurus, I do remember snickering gleefully when he locked Fred outside the front door.

Now, instead of yelling "Wilma!" at the top of our lungs, we

Grand Junction is a nirvana for dinosaur hunters.
Grand Junction Visitor & Convention Bureau

★ ★

humanoids can yell "Eureka!" as we unearth the sixty-five-million-year-old remains of Dino's relatives. Even amateurs like me are invited along on Grand Junction's paleontological expeditions.

Sponsored by the Museum of Western Colorado, the dinosaur digs allow wannabes to dig for, cast, and analyze real fossils. All paying guests get time in the field and in the museum's Dinosaur Journey learning lab. And, no, the museum is not just humoring volunteers. Government cuts have severely restricted money for paleontological research, so volunteers actually fill a much-needed gap.

Indeed. Several years ago a volunteer from Illinois unearthed the shoulder blade of a nodosaur, a brand-new species. Although it took six months to fully recover the spine, the armor, and the club tail, her discovery has gone down in the record books. So when I learned that an average of six new species are discovered each year, I had visions of *Newsweek* covers and the new groutasaurus. But then I was told that in the paleontological community, naming a dinosaur after its finder was considered "poor form."

Grand Junction is a gold mine for dinosaur coroners. This fossil-laden wedge of the West lies within the massive Morrison geological formation, a crusty, twisted region that allowed ancient layers of the earth to grind to the surface. In the last hundred years, more than fifty kinds of dinosaurs have been discovered there, including the larg-est (the five-story ultrasaurus), the smallest (it's the size of a chicken), and the brachiosaurus that now resides in Chicago's Field Museum.

It's not unusual for volunteers to unlodge petrified footprints, eggs, nests, and everything from diplodocus to camarasaurus. Sometimes, however, it can be challenging to identify your catch. Unlike on *CSI* where research is done on warm bodies, research here is done on deaths that are sixty-five million years old. Unfortunately, all the wit-nesses are dead, and the evidence has been left out in the rain.

The Museum of Western Colorado offers one- and five-day digs. To dig them up on the Web, go to www.museumofwesternco.com/dino-digs, or call (888) 488-DINO.

★ ★

Back to the Future

There's a 140-million-year-old watering hole west of Grand Junction at Rabbit Valley. In the good old days, it provided respite for camarasaurus, diplodocus, iguanodons, apatosaurus, brachiosaurus, and lots of other dinosaurs. Today, thanks to the Museum of Western Colorado and the Bureau of Land Management, you can visit the watering hole via a 1.5-mile loop that's called the Trail Through Time. Brochures explaining each stop of the interpretive trail are available at the museum and at the site.

Lyme-Aid
Heeney

Of all the things we lost on September 11, 2001, the annual Heeney Tickfest surely wasn't the most important. But when Homeland Security closed the area below the Green Mountain Dam where the festival was always held, it was a sad day nonetheless. Up until that day when the Bureau of Reclamation felt compelled to close the area to the public, the Heeney Tickfest raised money for the Lower Blue Volunteer Fire Department. As fund-raisers go, it had no peers. Where else would people pay to buy rocks, smash plates, vote for Tick Queen and King, or enter parades dressed as "Luna-ticks" or "Scien-ticks"?

The Tickfest started as a community party when the population of Heeney was around fifty, which probably included some dogs. It honored a pioneer woman's successful comeback from a nasty bug bite.

For the first year after the cancellation of the Heeney Tickfest, town activists tried an alternative fund-raiser called the Not-the-2002-

★ ★

Heeney-Tick-Fest. It had a garage sale, but somehow it didn't have the same appeal as the parade, the Firefighters Olympics, and the trophy won by the king and queen on which they had to engrave their own names.

To get to Heeney, take CO 9 about 18 miles north of the I-70 Silverthorne/Dillon exit 205. And if you want to reminisce about the former Tickfest, contact Keats Ann Scott at (970) 724-9307.

In Heeney they don't mind being called "Luna-ticks."
Keats Ann Scott/Colorado Dreams

Found Your Marbles

Michelangelo was about 400 years too early. If he'd been around in 1873 when an entire mountainside of marble was discovered in central Colorado, he'd have surely ditched the inferior Carrera mines and gone for this marble, which at the time was described as "gigantic, remarkable, flawless, and immense."

In the years preceding World War I, the boomtown named Marble (what else?) had a population of 1,400, many of whom were Italian immigrants who worked in either the Yule Marble Mine or the finishing mill, the world's largest. Developed by Colonel Channing Meek with a little investment help from the Rockefellers, the Yule mine provided the marble for the Lincoln Memorial, the Tomb of the Unknown Soldier, the New York Municipal Building, and the Montana State Capitol, to name just a few.

But being located at 9,300 feet above sea level, the mine and the town had a few economic setbacks, like on May 20, 1912, when the mill was completely wiped out by a huge snowslide, or later that same summer, when Colonel Meek was killed after jumping from a runaway trolley. After the last of the Lincoln Memorial stone was shipped in 1917 and most of the Italian workers had left to fight the war in Europe, the mine barely limped along until it finally closed in 1941.

This story does have a happy ending, however. Not only did the Lakewood Girl Scout troop get the Colorado legislature to name Yule marble as the state rock, but the Yule Marble Mine reopened in 1990, the site where the finishing mill was located made the National Register of Historic Places, and today there's a Marble Institute of Colorado that offers sculpting classes right where it all began.

Vertical Golf

Kremmling

The renowned Kremmling Cliff Golf Classic has yet to attract the likes of Tiger Woods or Phil Mickelson. Instead, it pits such golfers as Bob Szulczewski and Thad and Zach School against the whims of gravity. With three tee boxes atop the 3,000-foot Kremmling Cliffs, these fearless golfers drive golf balls at nine rigged holes at the cliff's base along Muddy Creek.

Over the years targets have included everything from a beat-up RV to a canoe to a dump truck. But even a dump truck's hard to

But I can't see the flag!
Jean Landess/*Middle Park Times*

★ ★

hit when you're teeing off the side of a cliff, a cliff that can only be accessed by a 7-mile dirt road. Just ask the folks at Grand Elk Golf Course, who offer a free set of clubs to anyone nabbing a hole in one. Unfortunately, the closest ball on record is still 6 inches short.

Remember how I told you Kremmling Cliff Golf Classic was renowned? Here's why: At the 2004 Cliff Golf Classic, nineteen golfers were struck by lightning at the same time, a statistical impossibility. Thankfully, they all survived, but not without two of them dying for a minute or two until the defibrillator brought them back to life and another four being helicoptered to a Denver hospital. *National Geographic* even staged a half-hour reenactment.

Across the Buddhaverse
Red Feather Lakes

Located at the confluence of three northern Colorado valleys is the largest Buddhist monument in North America. It's 108 feet tall, features a 40-foot gold-plated statue of the big guy himself, and attracts believers and nonbelievers alike who travel to the remote 600-acre Shambhala Mountain Center to "ooh" and "aah" the type of architectural wonder you normally see only in Tibet. The Great Stupa of Dharmakaya That Liberates Upon Seeing, as it is known, took fourteen years to complete, the Dalai Lama himself came to bless it, and the skull of the guy who inspired it is buried inside the stupa along with thousands of other religious relics.

How did this spired Buddhist shrine get from the Bodhi tree to the landlocked rocky pine forests of northern Colorado? Chögyam Trungpa Rinpoche, whose skull serves as a sort of cosmic mascot, was one of the first lamas to introduce Buddhism to the West. He moved to Boulder in the early 1970s, translated ancient Tibetan works into English, and launched a widely successful meditation movement. He was also known to drink heavily, fly around in helicopters, and pal around with hippies, beats, and his close friend Allen Ginsberg.

When he died in 1987, Rinpoche's Boulder devotees wanted to do

It's not the economy, stupa.
Shambhala Mountain Center

★ ★

something to acknowledge the brilliance of his teachings. Building a stupa, a moundlike structure containing Buddhist relics, is a powerful way to gain Buddhist brownie points. Believers claim stupas promote harmony, prosperity, longevity, good health, peace, and freedom from ignorance. And if all that weren't enough, they bring blessings to the environment where they're built, to those who build them, and to those who visit and venerate them—a win-win if ever there was one. Joshua Mulder drew plans for the Great Stupa the following year and, after turning down a job with NASA, has been artistically directing it ever since.

The stupa has inlaid granite and quartz floors, detailed Tibetan ceiling paintings, and a 110-foot life force pole with thousands of 24-karat gold inscribed prayers. It is expected to last for a minimum of one hundred years.

Besides the out-of-the-way $2.5 million stupa, Shambhala Mountain Center, pegged by *USA Today, Travel & Leisure,* and *Forbes* as one of the country's top 10 meditation centers, also offers such classes as Zen archery, Jewish mysticism, Chinese qigong, and yoga.

The Great Stupa of Dharmakaya, c/o Office of Development, 4921 CR 68C, Red Feather Lakes, CO 80545; (888) STUPA-21; www.shambhalamountain.org.

Monument to Why Ponzi Schemes Don't Pay
Redstone

Barack Obama would like this entry. It provides audacious hope that one of these days all the sacks of Ponzi-selling fat cats will finally get their comeuppance. In Redstone, where Norman Schmidt, his wife, Jannice, and five of their closest criminals bilked a thousand investors of more than $56 million, there's a historic castle that stands as a beacon of hope that, indeed, using proceeds differently than what you promise investors will lead to bad things. In May 2003 the feds seized the castle that the seven crooks bought illegally with trusting investors' money. I'm happy to report they were convicted a year later

Before Bernie Madoff.
Sue McEvoy

by a federal grand jury, and all seven are serving time for securities fraud, conspiracy, money laundering, and a few dozen other felony counts. The one hundred-plus-year-old castle was purchased at an IRS auction by an honest man who lets the Redstone Historical Society offer horse-drawn sleigh tours of the place.

But maybe we should rewind a bit. The opulent, forty-two-room Redstone Castle was built in 1897 by industrialist John Cleveland Osgood, who also financed eighty-four Swiss-style cottages, a school, a clubhouse, and a forty-room inn for the coal miners and cokers who worked his mines. The 21,000-square-foot castle, where Osgood entertained Teddy Roosevelt, John D. Rockefeller, J. P. Morgan, and other titans, has gold-leaf ceilings, maroon velvet walls, mahogany fireplaces, and Tiffany chandeliers. So you can see why Schmidt and

★ ★

his merry band of crooks might be greedy enough to want to own it. Luckily, the feds stood up for the little guys they conned and threw them out just in time for the Tudor-style castle to be used in the filming of the 2006 movie *The Prestige,* starring Hugh Jackman, Michael Caine, Christian Bale, and Scarlett Johansson.

Redstone Castle is located at 58 Redstone Boulevard; (970) 963-9656; www.redstonecastle.us.

Don't Blink or You'll Miss It

Rifle

When Christo hung 23 miles of fabric in Central Park in February 2005, he was a household name. But when the Bulgarian-born artist began hanging fabric in Colorado back in 1972, people weren't quite sure what to think of him.

"You want to what?" was the most common response. After all, it's not everyday you get artists asking to hang bright orange curtains across a canyon, especially one that's 1,250 miles long. Figure in the cost ($700,000) and the time (two years and four months to get it all ready), and it's no wonder people were scratching their heads.

Just the same, they lined up to help the then-unknown artist string the nylon curtain across Rifle Gap in the Grand Hogback mountain range. On August 10, 1971, at exactly 11 a.m., a group of thirty-five construction workers and sixty-four college students tied down the last of twenty-seven ropes that secured the 142,000-square-foot curtain across CO 325.

The artist was so elated (never mind that weather forecasters were predicting gale winds of 60 miles an hour) and the workers so glad to let go of the 9-ton curtain that they threw the overjoyed artist plum into Rifle Creek. He barely had time to dry off before the installation, designed to stay put for a month, had to be taken down. Even though it lasted a short twenty-eight hours, Valley Curtain, as it was known, was one of Christo's most famous projects, the first big one that launched his illustrious career.

★ ★

Valley Curtain hung 7 miles north of Rifle on CO 325 between Grand Junction and Glenwood Springs in the Grand Hogback mountain range.

Rule Number One: Avoid Snowbanks
Steamboat Springs

So you grew up in Miami, and you've just been transferred to Alaska? Or you're from Galveston, and that gal you met on match.com, the cute one from Minneapolis, still insisits on a visit in January? If it's

At this driving school, the tracks are groomed with 80,000 gallons of water.
Bridgestone Winter Driving School

your first time, driving on snow and ice can be hair-raising at best, dangerous if you're not quite so lucky.

Perhaps you can con your Alaska-transferring boss or your match .com love to enroll you in the Bridgestone Winter Driving School in Steamboat Springs. The only school of its kind in the country, BWDS (for motorheads in the know) has classrooms in downtown Steamboat, a 400-acre driving range, and a harrowing ice track.

Students learn the physics of driving, as well as the steering and braking techniques for slippery surfaces and the driving lines that are possible through snowy curves and corners. The course is downright nasty, with ten serious corners, and to make sure it's truly challenging, it's groomed each season with more than 80,000 gallons of water. To keep it slick, of course.

BWDS operates seven days a week between December and February. If the weather is bad enough, it stays open through March.

For information on slinging slush with the best of them, call the Bridgestone Winter Driving School at (800) WHY-SKID; write 1850 Ski Time Square Drive, Steamboat Springs, CO 80477; or go to www.winterdrive.com.

Honey, I Unshrunk the Toys
Steamboat Springs

As the saying goes, the only difference between men and boys is the size of their shoes and the price of their toys. At Dig This!, a giant sandbox in Steamboat Springs, the toys are real bulldozers, excavators, and cranes, and the "boys" are corporate executives, high-dollar skiers, and other adults who pay between $450 (half-day) and $700 (full-day) to play in a ten-acre sandbox.

It all started three years ago when Ed Mumm, a New Zealand transplant, rented an excavator to clear the land he'd recently purchased 6 miles west of town. Scooping dirt and VW bug–sized boulders, Mumm had a revelation: "This is the most fun I've had since grade school." A half million dollars later, Mumm now spends his

Haulin' ass . . . phalt.
Dig This!

days passing out orange vests to wealthy thrill seekers who come to dig holes, hoist, and raze at the fantasy playground he constructed.

His Dig This! fleet includes a 6-ton skid-steer loader, a 115-horse-power excavator, and Caterpillar's D5G bulldozer, described as 10 tons of glinting muscle. Mumm feels confident that his super-size Tonka toys tap an unrequited vein of the American psyche. He calls it the first—and so far only—heavy equipment playground in the United States.

"I can guarantee you that 30 to 40 percent of all adults who pass a construction site think, 'Man, I wish I could have a go at that,'" says Mumm, who also raises reindeer on his property. "I think that, sub-consciously, we never grew out of our sandboxes."

Mumm picks up his wannabe heavy equipment operators in

downtown Steamboat. He ferries them to the overgrown sandbox in a shrink-wrapped van. Instructors start with safety briefings before guiding them through such exercises as digging ditches, stacking I-beams, and pushing boulders around obstacle courses.

Mumm figures Dig This! is the next ropes course and hopes to sell franchises for the corporate bonding experience that he claims builds self-confidence, balance, and hand-eye coordination.

"Throttling up a powerful engine and sculpting mounds of earth is very empowering," he says.

And while insurance companies balked at providing coverage, all their executives came out to play with the equipment.

Dig This! is located at 1169 Hilltop Parkway, Suite 201; (970) 367-4402; www.digthis.info.

Big Bang Barbecue
Upper Colorado River

Polish astronomer Nicolaus Copernicus pissed a lot of people off back in 1543 when he figured out that the earth, rather than being the center of the universe, was just another ordinary planet orbiting the sun. Too bad he wasn't a white-water rafter. Then he would have known that the center of the universe is located along the banks of the Upper Colorado River in a former hippie colony known as Rancho Del Rio. Or at least that's what the hand-painted wooden sign says. The center of the universe doubles as KK's BBQ, a little outdoor, five-stool bar and grill with giant jars of homemade pickles, pots of home-made barbecue sauce, and slices of the best homemade pie this side of Grandma's house.

Eponymous proprietor Karen Gravenhorst, who can't remember what the second K stands for, serves burgers, Polish sausage, and bar-becued beef ribs, slathered in a sauce bequeathed to her by an old-time barbecue master. "We just deal with the basics. No fancy stuff, but it's good chow," KK says. "It was my dream to own a little diner. I just didn't expect to do it for twenty years."

★ ★

Center of the universe or not, KK is a regular one-woman act, entertaining her customers, most of whom have shown up to raft, kayak, and tube the mighty Colorado, with her jokes, stories, and more than twenty bells that hang from her outdoor kiosk. KK's is open Saturday, Sunday, and Monday between Memorial Day and the last Sunday in September, and while she has a skeletal Web site (www.kkbbq.com), she claims it's better to show up and experience the real thing.

Rancho Del Rio has cabins, a campground, an assortment of trailers and kayaks, canoes, and tubes for rent. Write to them at 4199 Trough Road, Bond, CO 80423; call (970) 653-4431, or visit www.ranchodelrio.com.

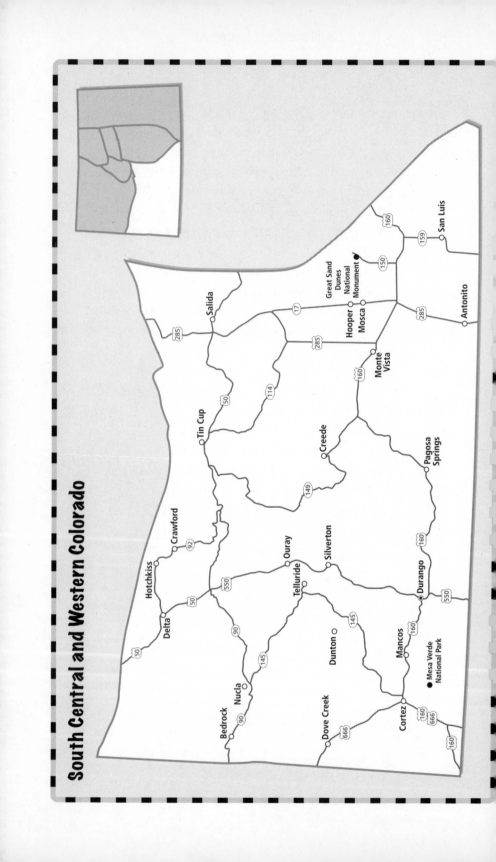

South Central and Western Colorado

9

South Central and Western Colorado

It's hard to *believe any place could be this beautiful. I mean, even Princess Diana had an eating disorder. But as far as I can tell, there isn't so much as a single yard in the region covered in this chapter that's anything but drop-dead-take-your-breath-away gorgeous.*

And that's not even what I'm supposed to be writing about. This is a book about quirky characters and oddball attractions, after all, the kinds of things that don't get put in tourist brochures.

Luckily, the area covered in this chapter also happens to be plum full of weirdness. I mean, there's an 8-mile beach wedged right between two mountain ranges, a tower for spotting UFOs, a three-story castle made entirely out of beer cans, and an alligator farm with 450 11-foot reptiles. And that, my friends, is just the beginning.

★ ★

One Hundred Cans of Beer on the Wall

Antonito

You might suspect a guy who builds a three-story castle out of beer cans would guzzle a lot of brewskis. But Donald Espinoza, who has devoted the past twenty-five years of his life to constructing what he calls the "Jesus Castle" out of thousands of beer cans, hubcaps, and anything else he can pull out of the dump across the street, says he swore off the stuff years ago. He prefers marijuana, which he claims gives him inspiration. In fact, a sign inside the red-willow gate leading into his unique beer castle complex reads TOBACCOO IS KILLS [sic] and MARY JANE IS HEALING.

Besides the misspelled sign, Espinoza's castle complex has a 6-foot cross made of Keystone Light cans, a beehive oven with marbles depicting the plane crashes of 9/11, an apricot grove, a Virgin Mother bathtub, and the castle's king and queen made of overlapping circles of hubcaps.

Though the stories vary (some say his mother's repeated demands to do something about empty beer cans in the yard instigated the project), Espinoza, a Vietnam vet, says the elaborate castle is a memorial to his mother, Margaret Trujillo Espinoza, who died in 1992, and his best friend, Gilbert "Pancho" Salazar, who was killed in Vietnam five days before his tour of duty was to end.

When he's not adding new junk to his castle, Espinoza runs, his gray, frizzy hair pulled back in braids. In fact, his Sunday morning route takes him past all the bars in Antonito in search of Saturday night's empties. In the summertime, when the Cumbres & Toltec Scenic Railroad is running, he's apt to don a headband and breechcloth and race bareback on his horse alongside the train, whooping for the benefit of the tourists.

Ask him his real name (he goes by Cano) or his age or about Vietnam, and he'll just stare off at the Sangre de Cristos, stone silent until you get back on a subject more suitable of his time. Like philosophy. "Life is short," he says. "You can live it hot or lukewarm. I'm going to stay warm all the time."

★ ★

Cano's castle is located in Antonito, a crumbling Spanish town on US 285, approximately 30 miles south of Alamosa and an hour north of Taos, New Mexico. Even though there's no street address, you can't really miss it; it's the only three-story building in town. Look for the signs DISTRIBUTE THE WEALTH and BROKEN TREATIES.

Flintstones, Meet the Flintstones
Bedrock

It's a place right out of history, all right. Although the population in its namesake town rings in at a paltry 232 folks, the Bedrock Store, an old-time Western supply center that has been around since 1881, has everything a biker, a rafter, or a hiker could ever need. Of course, that's the main clientele of this little store on CO 90 in the Paradox Valley.

Whether you need a patch for your bike tire, information on rafting conditions, or an ice-cream bar, this little store with walls made from uncoursed native stone is sure to have it. It also has decorative barrels full of antlers and homemade honey-glazed beef jerky.

When it was first built, the Bedrock Store served the local ranching community as a post office and a general merchandise store. It was the only store within 30 miles. Of course, nowadays the post office, which has since acquired its own location, gets mail addressed to Fred and Wilma Flintstone, as well as things like an actual rock mailed from England. The old postmaster used to answer all the Flintstones' letters (there wasn't cable TV back then), but since he retired, the new postmaster isn't quite as diligent a correspondent.

The Bedrock Store's biggest claim to fame, however, is a starring role in the movie *Thelma and Louise.* Louise (played by Susan Sarandon) called the FBI agent (played by Harvey Keitel) from the little store in Unaweep Canyon.

The Bedrock Store is located at 9812 Highway 90 in the tiny town of Bedrock; phone (970) 859-7395.

★ ★

Massive Cover-up
Cortez

There's murder. There's intrigue, but, thankfully, the massive cover-up in Cortez is only a rug. Not that the world's largest Two Grey Hills rug is anything to sneeze at. Most of the Navajo weavings known as Two Grey Hills are used as wall hangings. A 5-by-7-foot Two Grey Hills would be rare enough, but the one in Cortez at the Notah Dineh Trading Company is 12 by 18 feet. It took more than three years to weave, and the trader who commissioned Navajo artist Rachel Curley to create this unusual rug was murdered before it ever got completed.

Two Grey Hills rugs, for those of you who don't frequent Indian trading posts, are the Cadillacs of Navajo rugs. They're bordered rugs that use all-natural gray and brown wools. Because the weave is fine and very intricate, it's not something just anybody can throw together. To give you some perspective, a weft (that's the threads running across and woven into the warp threads) count of fifty per inch is considered a high-quality rug. A weft count of eighty or more qualifies the rug as a tapestry. Two Grey Hills rugs have counts of 120 or more.

Willard Leighton, who was known as Chis Chilly (curly hair) to the Navajo, contracted Rachel, who hails from a long line of rug makers, to weave the one-of-a-kind rug in 1957. Before she could finish it (remember it took three years), Willard was murdered, so when Rachel finally completed the rug in 1960, Willard's brother, Bob, who wanted the rug but couldn't afford to keep it, took it on a trading trip. He talked the owner of the Quarter Circle Ranch in Montana into exchanging his fine Persian rugs for the Navajo equivalent. Bob never forgot about that rug, always hoping he'd see it again.

Thirty years later, an Indian art dealer contacted Bob about this rare masterpiece rug that he'd found in Santa Barbara. Seems it was too large for the home it was purchased for. Sure enough, it was the rug Bob's brother, Willard, had commissioned. After touring the country in an exhibit of Navajo weavings, the expensive rug is finally resting in Bob's family's Notah Dineh Trading Company in Cortez.

Cortez's Notah Dineh, which has the largest collection of Navajo rugs in the Four Corners, is located at 345 West Main Street; phone (800) 444-2024.

Bubble the Pleasure, Bubble the Fun
Crawford

Environmentalist Ed Eaton has made several solar-powered bubble machines, including one that blows 10,000 bubbles per minute. When he tested that model on the main street of Carbondale, traffic ground to a halt. Whether drivers stopped to witness the novelty or were too afraid to drive through that many uncontained solar bubbles, they didn't say.

Eaton's current bubble machine uses a small solar-powered 12-volt gear motor along with a small blower fan, and he made it not because he believes solar energy and other renewable energy sources are the wave of the future. "Solar," Eaton says, "is important because it's a large piece of the sustainable living puzzle. It allows us to cook, heat living spaces, purify water, and farm without using up precious resources." He's currently converting a diesel school bus into a solar kitchen so he can take "his show" on the road. He plans to sell "hempsickles" and spread the word about the importance of renewable energy.

Ed Eaton can be reached at 1920 Black Canyon Road, Crawford, CO 81415; (970) 921-5529.

More Than One Way to Skin a Cat
Creede

Even though the editors at *Mother Earth News* called Creede one of the best places to live in North America, only 400 or so folks have taken them up on the offer. With a tax base like that, city planners knew it wasn't going to be easy to raise the money for a new fire station. Still, since the entire town burned to the ground just three years after it was established in 1889, it was something they felt forced to propose.

Luckily, the innovative little town lifted itself above convention and came up with the novel idea of building their fire station into the side of a cliff. Using explosives rather than lumber, they blasted out 45-degree-angle rock stalls for the volunteer fire department's two fire trucks and inadvertently opened up a whole new trickle of revenue. In fact, so many tourists came to see the World's Only Underground Firehouse (the local 4-H Club gives tours) that they eventually decided to blast another tourist attraction—an underground mining museum.

The World's Only Underground Firehouse is located along Willow Creek Road on the north end of town. The Creede/Mineral County Chamber of Commerce can be reached at (800) 327-2102.

Tipi or Not Tipi
Delta

Martha Stewart may know how to make a lovely autumn floral swag and how to whip up a replica of the Vatican from sugar cubes, but I'll bet she doesn't know the finer points of tipi etiquette. That's something you can learn at the Council Tree Pow Wow & Cultural Festival held every September in Delta.

A celebration of Ute culture, the festival features an Indian market and a tipi village across the river from the 200-year-old cottonwood tree where Ute chiefs once smoked the peace pipe. The crash course in tipi etiquette, which includes, among other things, not staring at strangers, thanking the Great Spirit for each meal, and leaving when the host cleans his pipe, is available to anyone wanting to rent a tipi in Tipi Village.

Of course, first you have to fill out an official tipi application that sounds an awful lot like an apartment lease agreement. But at least you get your own parking pass.

For information on Tipi Village, which includes a tipi from the

Defying Mathematics

Multiplying loaves and fishes is one thing. But in Creede, with a population of less than 400, the world-famous repertory theater manages to sell 20,000 tickets every season. How do they do that? By winning kudos from everyone from *USA Today* (their reviewer dubbed Creede Repertory Theater "one of the 10 great places to see the lights way off Broadway") to *Rocky Mountain News,* who said, "No wonder the *Denver Post* calls it 'a miracle in the mountains.'" Creede Repertory Theater is at 124 North Main Street and can be reached at (719) 658-2540 or (866) 658-2540; www.creederep.org.

movie *Dances with Wolves* and one painted by Disney artists for the grand opening of their animated feature *Pocahontas,* check out the Web site at www.counciltreepowwow.org.

Bean There, Done That

Dove Creek

Pueblo psychologist Chester "Buck" Weimer could be the poster boy for "necessity being the mother of invention." In 1997 his wife developed Crohn's disease, an inflammatory bowel disease that, while not fatal, often comes with an annoying side effect: flatulence. After much experimentation, Weimer developed and patented a pair of airtight underwear with an absorbent charcoal filter. In other words, "it made car trips with my wife more pleasant," he says. So far, he has sold more than 10,000 pairs of the sound-dampening, air-diffusing, odor-removing briefs from the cellar of his Pueblo home.

Another Colorado remedy for what's also known as trouser coughs, air biscuits, cheese cutting, and short snorts is Anasazi beans,

★ ★

Beans, beans, the magical food. The more you eat, the more you need these underwear.
Courtesy of Buck Weimer, Under-tec

a purplish red-and-white relative of the pinto bean that contains 75 percent less of the complex carbohydrates that cause, shall we just say, gastric distress. Adobe Milling, an heirloom bean company in Dove Creek, the "Pinto Bean Capital of the World," has been selling Anasazi beans (and other so-called boutique beans) since 1983.

The Anasazi bean, also called Aztec bean, cave bean, and Jacob's cattle, is a 1,500-year-old bean that, according to popular lore, was unearthed by an archaeological team from UCLA that was looking for remains of pygmy elephants. The beans, one of the few crops culti-vated by the Anasazi, were allegedly discovered in a clay pot sealed with pine tar. Surprisingly, the beans still germinated a millennium and a half later, a mystery nearly as clouded as the missing Four Cor-ners tribe itself.

Besides the lack of fart-inducing chemicals, the Anasazi bean that Adobe Milling quickly trademarked and began shipping around the world requires no soaking and cooks in two-thirds the time of an ordinary pinto bean.

For more information about the beans, contact Adobe Milling, P.O. Box 596, Dove Creek, CO 81324; (800) 542-3623; www.anasazi beans.com. To contact Buck Weimer about his amazing underwear, visit www.under-tec.com.

There's More

Located 8 miles from the Utah border, Dove Creek also has these amenities:

- **Lots of pinkish clothes. The reason pinto beans thrive in Dove Creek is because the soil there is high in iron content. While good for bean cultivating, it tends to stain laundry a faintish red color.**

- **Greased pig chasing. At Dove Creek's annual Fourth of July Pick n' Hoe, kids of all ages chase greased pigs. The prize? The oinker itself.**

- **A huge deposit of uranium. Unfortunately, it's too expensive to mine.**

- **Tell-all books. If you can get your hands on a copy of *The Crow Flies Crooked,* a deliciously wicked novel loosely based on former residents of Dove Creek, you can sell it for nearly one hundred times its original purchase price. Even though it won a 1966 silver medal from the Commonwealth Club, its publication didn't sit well with locals who recognized themselves in its pages. Its author, Jack Kisling, owner of the rural weekly *Dove Creek Press,* tried to pull it off as fiction, but that didn't stop the town from purchasing all the copies they could find and destroying them. That's why the book, a rarity, currently sells for $179 on Amazon.**

★ ★

Ghost Town Spa
Dunton

In the 1890s the town of Dunton had a population of 500, most of whom worked the nearby mines. By 1918 the mine shut down, and Dunton, like many Colorado towns, became a ghost town. Although it had a short reincarnation in the 1970s as a hangout for hippies, bikers, and nude volleyball types who traded beers for dips in the hot springs, its bordello, saloon, and cabins basically sat boarded up for seventy-five years.

In 1994 a German and an Austrian skiing in Telluride heard that the entire town was selling for about the same price as a condo in Aspen. Fifteen minutes after finding the place (it's a good forty-five

Bubbles for the rich and famous.
Dunton Hot Springs

214

minutes from the nearest non–ghost town), the European friends decided to snatch it up, battered facade be damned.

After funneling $3 million into the place (each of the twelve cabins was decorated by a Munich art dealer with a monstrous budget and extremely good taste), they found that they'd fallen so madly in love with their "Vild Vest" ghost town that rather than sell lots, as they originally intended, they'd keep the whole 187 acres and rent it out as a $10,000 a night corporate retreat center.

Before long, they opened their ghost town spa to individual guests, including Daryl Hannah, Tom Cruise, and Ralph Lauren, who happens to own a vast acreage nearby. The yoga room is a former Pony Express stop; the bathhouse still has bullet holes; the library is an old barn furnished with distressed-leather armchairs and bearskin rugs; one of the four hot springs (two indoors, two out) is located in a tipi; and the dining hall is the town's old saloon, with a long wood bar scratched with names of people who have tipped the bottle there. The name of Butch Cassidy, who allegedly stayed in Dunton after robbing his first bank in nearby Telluride, is one of the autographs.

Each of the twelve restored cabins, although postcard imperfect on the outside, is tremendously luxurious on the inside, with African textiles, baronial antiques, broadband Internet, radiant floor heating, and hundreds of thousands of dollars of art. No wonder Herbert Ypma, the guy behind the chintz-free *Hip Hotels* series, picked Dunton Hot Springs as one of his all-time top 20.

Dunton Hot Springs can be reached via a 22-mile dirt road off CO 145. For information, write to P.O. Box 818, Dolores, CO 81324; call (970) 882-4800, or visit www.duntonhotsprings.com.

Academy Award–Winning B&B
Durango

Normally, I'm not the bed-and-breakfast type. I love the breakfast part—at home I normally get Cheerios. But the bed part, the part where I "ooh" and "aah" over Victorian lace, antique ironing boards,

★ ★

Once a flophouse, the Rochester Hotel is now a stellar B&B.
Leavitt Studios

and the cute little nineteenth-century wash basin—you know, the one I'm expected to wash my face in the next morning—is more than I can generally muster.

However, the Rochester in Durango gets a hearty thumbs up because each of its fifteen rooms is named for a movie, usually a Western, that was filmed in the area. There's the *Support Your Local Gunfighter* room, the *Butch Cassidy and the Sundance Kid* room, the *City Slickers* room (it even has a painting of Norman, the two-week-old Jersey cow that adopted Billy Crystal), and so on. The appropriate movie poster framed in marquee lights hangs outside each door.

More than seventy movies have been shot in the Durango area. In fact, in 1952 a monument naming it "The Hollywood of the Rockies" was dedicated by Jimmy Stewart and Janet Leigh, who were both in town making *The Naked Spur.* It was the fourteenth movie shot there in five years, many of which won Academy Awards.

The craze started back in the early 1940s, when 20th Century Fox honcho Darryl Zanuck and his family vacationed at a local dude ranch. They were so taken with the area that in 1948 Zanuck sent a production company to film *Sand,* the first in a long stream of movies shot in and around Durango.

The list of stars that tromped through Durango includes not only Jimmy Stewart and Janet Leigh, but also John Wayne, Clark Gable, Marlon Brando, and an unknown named Marilyn Monroe. She had a bit part as a chorus girl in 1950's *Ticket to Tomahawk.* One day after filming, a local Durango team challenged the film crew to a charity softball game. Even though home plate was blown up, Indians chased umpires, and stuntmen faked all sorts of antics, it was Marilyn's base hit that stole the show. Her blue jeans fell to her ankles, and by the time she reached first base, she was wearing little but her black lace underwear.

Unfortunately, Diane Wildthang and Kirk Komick, the mother-and-son duo who own the Rochester, couldn't track down the underwear, but they did manage to find dozens of other props, photos, and lobby cards that are displayed throughout the property. They have all fifteen movies that the rooms are named for on video (you can even watch them on the lobby's big-screen TV), and Diane's husband, an aspiring screenwriter with ten scripts under his belt, has even written a book about Durango's movie history.

Of course, the hotel itself has a plot that deserves two thumbs up. The two-story brick building has been in near-continuous operation since it was built in 1882, and, yes, it has hosted its share of gunfighters, miners, saloon girls, and other assorted rowdies. It even had a bit part in the 1972 Western *When the Legends Die.* Richard Widmark and Frederic Forrest duke it out in the room that's now being used as the Rochester kitchen. That's one of the movies I haven't seen, but I'll bet a lemon-ginger muffin or a short stack of pumpkin pancakes that it's being put to better use as the Rochester kitchen.

It's obvious the Komicks have a lot of fun with the property. The decor, which can best be described as cowboy funk, includes such whimsical touches as plants growing from cowboy boots and beat-up Stetsons thrown over hat stands. They host outdoor jazz in the beer garden and have a Rochester photo competition where guests win free prizes for sending in everything from Polaroids of Stitch, the resident terrier, to professional shots of the hotel with a horse and buggy out front.

They even pipe western music into the lobby. If I hadn't been so taken with the homemade brownies they put out each afternoon, I'd have probably found a partner and do-si-doed around the lobby.

For more information, contact the Rochester at 726 East Second Avenue, Durango, CO 81301; phone (970) 385-1920 or (800) 664-1920; www.rochesterhotel.com.

Wacky Reindeer Games
Durango

In a state filled with überathletes, it's refreshing to know there are still a few sports the rest of us can convincingly compete in. Cookie stacking, for example. It doesn't take tenacity or rippling muscles to build a tower of Oreos. Or Spam carving. To win this annual event, you simply must be able to turn a hunk of pink, unidentifiable meat into a three-headed dragon or a reproduction of the *Last Supper.* What's more, you get a whole ten minutes and a plastic knife to do it.

While a few of the events at Durango's annual Snowdown require a certain level of athletic skill (careening 40 miles an hour down a mountain in a kayak made for water, for instance), the majority of

Spam carving and cookie stacking are just two of the
many events at Durango's annual Snowdown.
Durango Area Tourism Office

the seventy zany events require creativity and derring-do. There are
prizes for best-dressed cat (dogs, too, are allowed in the feline fashion show), best art made from wine bottles, best ability to stuff you
and your closest friends into a port-a-potty (thirty-two is the record),
and dozens of other fascinating contests. The polar beer plunge (no,
that's not a typo) involves contestants diving into tanks of iced beer
to retrieve prizes. Spellabration tests three-person teams against some
of the most difficult words in the English language.

Snowdown, according to event organizers, was started back in
1975 "to alleviate toxic levels of cabins fever." It always has a theme
(like Yabadabadoorango or Disco Do It) chosen two years in advance,
and folks know they're in trouble when a boom box starts piping out
loud, obnoxious music. That means they're about to be hit in the face
with a cream pie.

For more information about Durango's Snowdown, check out the Web site www.snowdown.org, or call the tourism and convention department at (800) 525-8855.

Mr. Sandman, Bring Me a Dune
Great Sand Dunes National Monument

It has been called the world's largest ashtray. It would also make an excellent litter box for a very large house cat. But the Great Sand Dunes National Monument, an 8-mile beach that is admittedly a good 1,000 miles from the nearest ocean, deserves a far more complimentary description.

What's wrong with this picture?
National Park Service

★ ★

I mean, sure, you can't really wiggle your toes in the sand (we're talking temps of up to 140 degrees Fahrenheit on a hot summer day with no surf to dip your feet in), and you can't exactly set hiking records (remember that dream about walking in sand and getting nowhere?), but this place is truly like nowhere else in the world.

For one thing, how many beaches have you seen wedged between two huge mountain ranges? The Sangre de Cristos flank the east, and the San Juans border the west. Topping out at 750 feet, these sand dunes are the tallest on the North American continent, just a few feet shy of New York City's Met Life building.

And where else can you sled, ski, snowboard, snowshoe, and build sand castles all in one place?

Most of the park's 300,000 or so visitors come to conquer High Dune, the grandmother of all dunes, that at two steps forward, one step back can take a couple hours. Unless, of course, you're Jim Ryun, who trained for the 1968 Olympics by running straight up. How hard was it? "On a scale of 1 to 10, I'd rank it a 12," he said.

As for the 140-degree sand temps, fahgetaboutit. Park rangers carry spare socks.

To play Lawrence of Arabia, the Great Sand Dunes National Monument can be found 35 miles northeast of Alamosa, reached by US 160 and CO 150 from the south or from CO 17 and County Six Mile Lane (it's actually 8 miles) from the west. The phone number is (719) 378-6399.

If You Build It, Aliens Will Come

Hooper

When Judy Messoline and Stan Becker built their UFO Watchtower, it was mainly a gimmick, a way to attract tourists to their floundering cattle ranch outside Hooper. Sure, they'd heard rumors about unexplained phenomena in the area, but little did they suspect UFOs would actually show up.

It wasn't long before they added themselves to the ranks of

★ ★

The UFO Watchtower is out of this world.
Judy Messoline/UFO Watchtower

believers. Not only have they had four personal UFO sightings since the watchtower was erected in 2000, but they've also attracted trackers from around the world. Now, they even host a yearly UFO Olympics.

Although it's all done rather tongue-in-cheek (the signs leading to their campground are 8-foot red plywood alien cutouts, and for $2, you can have your photo taken with a stuffed alien), Judy and Stan can talk paranormal with the best of them.

And the best of them they get. In return for a free bumper sticker or Frisbee, Judy tapes visitors' tales of extraterrestrial encounters. She needn't bother with the rewards. Most of the tale tellers are so eager to be heard, they'd do it for free. There's a whole circuit of UFO believers who regularly traipse between the 125-mile-long San Luis Valley and Roswell, New Mexico, scene of an alleged 1947 UFO crash.

It all started after Judy's friend Babette called soon after she'd moved to Hooper and said, "Well, have you seen any?" "Any what?" replied Judy. Babette couldn't believe she hadn't heard about the UFOs in that area and suggested she read up on local investigator Christopher O'Brien, who wrote a book about cattle mutilations, mysterious helicopters, and oddly shaped aircraft hovering over the San Luis Valley. The book proved fortuitous, leading Judy and Stan to build the watchtower, open the campground, and start a peace garden with rocks from all over the world.

If you fancy camping next to the UFO Parking Only sign (it's on the other end of the parking lot from the UFO Handicapped Parking sign) or visiting the domed gift shop stocked with "alien dust" and big-eyed extraterrestrial dolls, the UFO Watchtower is located 2.5 miles north of Hooper on CO 17. Check out www.ufowatchtower.com, or call (719) 378-2296 for details.

Aloha, Colorado
Hotchkiss

If you've had trouble finding a Hawaiian shirt for your Irish setter, look no farther than Hotchkiss, Colorado, where Paradise on a Hanger sells not just one, but fifteen (count 'em) different Hawaiian shirts for your pooch. You can choose between tropical fish, flowers, palm trees, and exotic bird designs.

Paradise on a Hanger, the world's largest purveyor of mail-order Hawaiian shirts, also sells Hawaiian shirts for humans, which is no small accomplishment when you figure the family-run business is located at least 895 miles from the nearest ocean. In the mountains.

Started in 1989 by Steve and Curielle Duffy, Paradise on a Hanger also sponsors a Hawaiian Guy Hall of Fame, in which people send in photos of themselves wearing Hawaiian shirts in rather odd places. My favorite is the beer-bellied Hawaiian shirt in front of a historic statue.

Dog Ho.
Joel Kincaid/Paradise on a Hanger

The Duffys are walking advertisements for individualism and the pursuit of big dreams. Steve, who looks like he's on a perpetual vacation (he has been wearing nothing but Hawaiian shirts since he was twelve and bought a whole rack for 25 cents apiece at a garage sale in his hometown of Wheaton, Maryland), used to strut around his 3,000-square-foot warehouse with a parrot named Bubbles on his shoulder. But alas, Bubbles, at age sixteen, passed on to that great big fruit tree in the sky. And Curielle, when she's not helping Steve with the business, runs Camp Rock, an outdoor adventure camp.

To purchase a Hawaiian shirt for Rover or enter your photo in the Hall of Fame (you could even win a free shirt), visit Paradise on a Hanger at 360 West Bridge Street; call them at (800) 921-3050; or check out their Web site at www.hotshirts.com.

Open-Door Policy

Thanks to baby boomers with trust funds, mountain real estate is "Rocky Mountain high." In fact, there may be more "second homes" in Colorado than in any other state.

But before World War II, you didn't really need a second home, especially if you were hiking or visiting the mountains. People with Colorado cabins considered it their responsibility to leave them unlocked and even stocked with food. After all, you never knew when a storm might come up and some poor stranger might need sanctuary. To be fair, anyone who took advantage of this "open door" policy was honor bound to leave the cabin "better than they found it." Cabin owners never knew what kind of "new treats" they might find in their cabinets.

Alas, the Good Samaritan policy finally went the way of the Lindy thanks to ungrateful visitors who started vandalizing and robbing their generous hosts. Locksmiths were brought in, and the once-open cabins were shuttered and bolted tight. But one Texas owner of a cabin near Lake City got a bit overzealous. When he left in the fall, he rigged up a shotgun for anybody fool enough to enter his sanctum. Unfortunately, he forgot about his ingenious "alarm system," which worked just fine the next summer when he opened the door. Oops!

Weapons of Massive Destruction
Mancos

Unlike the world's largest rocking chair and the world's largest mural—both of which have aroused rather fierce competition—there is only one contender running for the world's largest arrow, and maybe that's because no one bothered to post a sign. Rather, the Navajos who

★ ★

erected the dozen or so giant arrows outside the Mud Creek Hogan on US 160 outside Mancos figured the humongous ammo speaks for itself.

The Rain of Giant Arrows was erected in 1959 to attract tourists to the trading post that sells rugs, beaded belts, handmade silver jewelry, and a bunch of Indian kitsch. The arrows are made from telephone poles stuck in the ground at a 45-degree angle and fitted with giant arrowheads.

Dwarfed by the big arrows are a few tipis. Definitely wouldn't have been a fair fight. The Mud Creek Hogan and its massive weapons are located at 38651 US 160 in Mancos; the phone number is (970) 533-7117.

Why We Have a National Antiquities Act

Mesa Verde National Park

One of the best places to view artifacts of Native American cliff dwellers is in . . . Helsinki, Finland.

Say what?

That's right, more than 600 artifacts from Colorado's own Mesa Verde currently reside in the National Museum of Finland in Helsinki. It seems one Gustaf Nordenskiold, a Swedish scholar, was the first scientist to excavate the cliff dwellings in southwest Colorado. Oh sure, the Wetherills from nearby Mancos had poked around Mesa Verde, but they were self-admitted cowboys and more than willing to lead the foreign archaeologist to the site.

Nordenskiold researched the area during the summer and autumn of 1891, writing an exhaustive account of the ruins and objects he uncovered during his excavations. His study, *The Cliff Dwellers of the Mesa Verde*, published in 1893, was one of the first scientific studies of North American archaeological sites.

Back then, America didn't have an Antiquities Act, so, after excavating several Mesa Verde sites, Nordenskiold did what any archaeologist would do: He crated up his finds (nine crates altogether) and shipped them home. Nordenskiold died an early death (he was only twenty-seven), and his nine crates of ancient artifacts somehow ended up in neighboring Finland at its National Museum. It's the largest group of ancient puebloan artifacts outside the United States.

Needless to say, there was a public outcry, which eventually inspired legislation that eventually resulted in the Antiquities Act of June 8, 1906, making "pot hunting" on federal lands illegal. Three weeks after that, Mesa Verde became a national park.

The National Museum of Finland is located at 34 Mannerheimintie, Helsinki, but if you'd rather visit Mesa Verde National Park, you can get information at www.nps.gov/meve; P.O. Box 8, Mesa Verde, CO 81330-0008; (970) 529-4465.

Bedtime Stories
Monte Vista

It's hard enough to find a drive-in theater these days. But finding a drive-in theater motel is even harder. In fact, it'd be downright impossible if it weren't for George Kelloff, an eighty-something movie buff who started the world's only motel where you can watch drive-in movies from your queen-size bed. He's been running the unique concept in motel management for forty-some years. Speakers on the wall pipe the audio into each room, and, if you can muster the energy, you can mosey down to the snack bar for Milk Duds and popcorn.

Kelloff, who opened a normal drive-in theater in Monte Vista back in 1959, used to lie in a hideaway bed in the kitchen of his home next door and watch the big screen he'd erected. One night he said to his wife, "This is really great. I think I'm going to open a whole motel with beds facing the screen." She, of course, thought he was crazy. But by 1964, the little motel was up and running.

Each of the motel's rooms is named after a movie star: the Tom Cruise room, the Mel Gibson room, and the John Wayne room, to name just a few. It's rumored the staff size up customers when they walk in the lobby, decide which star they most resemble, and then book them in that room. A short, dark-headed guy might get the

But does room service offer popcorn?
George Kelloff/Best Western Movie Manor Motor Inn

Danny DeVito room, for example. The whole place is loaded with movie star kitsch, including the walkway in front of the motel's restaurant where stars' names are etched into cement, almost looking like Grauman's Chinese Theatre East. The restrooms, of course, are labeled Actors and Actresses.

The Best Western Movie Manor Motor Inn is located at 2830 West US 160 in Monte Vista. For reservations or movie listings, call (719) 852-5921 or (800) 771-9468.

★ ★

See Ya Later, Alligator
Mosca

Mosca, Colorado, does not immediately spring to mind as a place to wrestle alligators. It's in the Rockies, at least a thousand miles from the nearest swamp. But show up at the Young residence, a geothermal tilapia fishing operation, and not only will you see gator wrasslin', as it's known in the biz, but you'll also see pythons, tortoises, and Sir Chomps O'Lot, the first alligator born in the San Luis Valley.

For $50, you can even take gator wrasslin' lessons, a four-hour course in how to confront an 11-foot, 500-pound reptile with eighty-two razor-sharp teeth. Of course, Gator Wrasslin' 101 starts with the little guys, the ones born last year that are only a foot long. "You have to work your way up to the big gators," says Jay Young, the head alligator wrestler.

At last count, there were 400 gators to choose from, a marked advance from the first 100 the Youngs bought in 1987 to clear up the leftover fillet problem. Before they knew what bit them, the Youngs were offering reptilian photo ops (an attendant lassoes a gator, drags it to a viewing area, and invites tourists to "sit down hard," keep their hands on its neck, and say "cheese") and alligator rodeos. August's Extreme Gator Elimination, for example, involves an obstacle course through the largest alligator pen.

The gift shop at Colorado Gators carries such novelties as alligator-shaped mugs, alligator-shaped squirt guns, and alligator roadkill baseball caps that share the brim with iguana, snapping turtle, beaver, and bull snake. Asking price for the baseball cap? $600.

Colorado Gators also offers an education program that teaches schoolkids about the biology, behavior, and ecological role of reptiles. Their specialty is teaching kids which reptiles make good pets and which ones will eventually eat your other pets.

Colorado Gators is located 17 miles north of Alamosa on CO 17. For more information, visit www.gatorfarm.com, or call (719) 378-2612.

★ ★

It Must Be the Water
Ouray

Plastics are the enemy. They leech into the products they contain, they let off gas (I'm not kidding, they let off a constant stream of unde-tectable fumes), and they're made from petroleum in a complicated process that creates major toxic waste. In a ranking by the Environ-mental Protection Agency of the top 20 chemicals in hazardous waste production, 5 of the top 6 are chemicals used in the plastics industry. What's more, you'd better like plastic, because it doesn't biodegrade and is going to be around at least 600 years longer than you are.

My biggest pet peeve, however, is bottled water, most of which is marketed by Pepsi (Aquafina) and Coca-Cola (Dasani). Maybe we could justify the 105 billion plastic water bottles produced each year and the 40 million bottles that end up in the landfill each day if their contents were truly more pure and healthy. But a huge percent of bottled waters comes straight from the same municipal water supply that pours from your tap. Yes, Pepsi, I'm talking to you.

From an environmental standpoint, bottled water is killing us.

Okay, so what's my point?

There's a company in Ouray that has figured out a better way to bottle water. In fact, BIOTA's water bottles (which are made from corn, not petroleum) break down as compost in less than three months. Furthermore, the water, unlike Dasani and Aquafina, which come from the same source as your tap, is pristine mountain-spring water. It really is better for you. It comes from the world's highest alpine springs, located above Ouray at 9,100 feet.

The unique bottles are the brainchild of Telluride resident David Zutler. When he decided to enter the burgeoning water market, he didn't want to use a plastic bottle made from oil. He spent six years researching the new renewable plastic resin, but it paid off. He's the first man to launch a beverage in a compostable bottle.

BIOTA, an acronym for Blame It On The Altitude, can be reached at (970) 728-6132, or visit their Web site at www.biotaspringwater.com.

Corny bottles.
Biota

Dog Eat Dog

Hard to believe a town as small as Nucla (pop. 734) could cause such a ruckus. But for years, this Western Slope burg that allegedly began as an experiment in communal living was the staging ground for an ongoing feud between hunters and animal rights activists. The hunters, armed with high-powered rifles and dressed in camouflage, trooped to Nucla from eleven states for the annual Top Dog World Prairie Dog Shoot, hosted each June by the Ten Ring Gun Club. They had a lot of fun, raised a lot of money (entry fee was $100 a hunter), got in a lot of "target" practice, and eradicated a lot of varmints that, as far as they were concerned, were nothing but a menace.

Animal rights supporters didn't share the sentiment. By 1989 they'd started a group called Prairie Dog Rescue, some 1,600 members strong, and before you knew it, everyone from the Sierra Club and the National Wildlife Federation to PETA and the Biodiversity Legal Foundation got involved. By June 1997 the Colorado Wildlife Commission limited the number of prairie dogs that could be killed by any one shooter in any one contest to five. The Varmint Militia, a group of forty-some hunters, so named to "piss off animal rights activists," claimed that didn't make for much of a competition, and the yearly event was soon canceled.

Though the Varmint Militia no longer holds contests, its members still shoot the animals for farmers and ranchers who want to get rid of them. It's a public service they perform for free. Says Mark Mason, who builds homes when he's not shooting prairie dogs, "Man is part of the ecosystem. For instance, we leave the carcasses for surrounding wildlife. We call ourselves the fast-food delivery service of the plains."

At last report, the militia still displays a stuffed prairie dog mascot named Daisy at gun shows.

★ ★

Ice Capades
Ouray

You might think that being spread-eagle on a 190-foot wall of ice or being slammed on the head by a cinder block of shattered glacier is the hardest part of ice climbing. But you'd be wrong.

The most challenging aspect of ice climbing is finding a place to do it. You either have to ignore no trespassing signs or hike so far into the wilderness that your only provisions are a sleeping bag and a backpack of freeze-dried stew. A bed and a flush toilet are definitely out of the question.

"I've sometimes walked a zillion miles and almost puked from exhaustion," says Ouray ice-climbing guide Mike O'Donnell, "all in search of 90 feet of frozen water."

That's why the Ouray Ice Park, the first park dedicated solely to the sport of ice climbing, is so unique. Not only does it have 1½ miles of ice, more than 150 routes, anchors for top roping, and every possible grade of climb, but it's a three-minute hike from the heart of Ouray, a funky, semirestored mining town where you can trade climbing tips over microbrews and then soak at one of the largest hot springs in the world.

Much of the nation's small and fanatical ice-climbing fraternity now winters in Ouray.

Climbers from as far away as Iceland, Australia, South America, and Europe have also come to rappel down gorge walls and scale frozen waterfalls. There's even a book called *Ouray Ice*.

"To an ice climber, hanging out in Ouray is akin to being a football fan and living next to Troy Aikman, Emmitt Smith, and Joe Namath," said Rahn Zaccari, an avid climber who moved to Ouray after the park was first opened.

Hollywood, too, has shown up. Budweiser and Chevrolet have filmed commercials in the ice park. And when *Batman & Robin* producers wanted a lair for Arnold Schwarzenegger's Mr. Freeze, they hired Mike O'Donnell to build a 300-foot ice wall, first in a Los

★ ★

Angeles meat locker and then in an old rock quarry in Vermont.

Beginners are welcome. In fact, there are so many guides in town that you can walk in and within hours be suited up and learning to duck walk. At the Ouray Ice Festival held every year over the long Martin Luther King Jr. weekend, beginners can take free classes on everything from the monkey hang to avalanche control.

You'll probably start on Schoolroom, the equivalent of a ski hill's bunny slope. From there, you'll move up to one of the higher-grade routes such as New Funtier, Southpark, maybe even Upper Bridge. Eventually, you might even want to lead a whole new route, which gives you the distinct honor of naming it. But don't take either task lightly: Coming up with a creative name can be almost as challenging as scaling a 120-foot icicle. For example, there's Aqua Velva, Root Canal, Bloody Sunday, Dancing with Penguins, Tangled up in Blue, and Stone Free.

Like the early days of skiing when locals tromped up mountains and built makeshift cabins, the Ouray Ice Park was built piece by piece by unpaid volunteers. On weekends, local climbers laid pipe, built catwalks, and installed nozzles. But unlike skiing, which eventually became pricey, the Ouray Ice Park will always and forever be free to anyone who is willing to defy gravity, nature, and their own humanness.

The Ouray Ice Park can be contacted at (970) 325-4288, or 306 Sixth Avenue, CO Ouray, 81427; www.ourayicepark.com.

And You Thought Freddy Krueger Was Bad
Ouray

Dan and Sandy Lingenfelter weren't the ghost-believing type when they first came to Ouray. Dan was an investment banker and Sandy a legal secretary before they decided to buy the St. Elmo, a restored turn-of-the-century B&B.

But after lights kept getting mysteriously turned on and off in the B&B's nine bedrooms and the hotel register kept getting inexplicably turned around, they decided to rethink their skepticism. They even consulted with a psychic who stayed at their inn.

Turns out that Kitty Heit, the frontier entrepreneur who built the St. Elmo back in 1892 as a boardinghouse for miners, had a son. His name was Freddy Porter, and let's just say he wasn't a happy camper. The alcoholic ne'er-do-well gambled away his life's savings in a Telluride saloon and came home to Momma, where he shot himself in Room 5 of her boardinghouse.

Although Freddy is still around, the psychic instructed the Lingenfelters to put Epsom salt in the windows, which has given the old boy his peace.

The St. Elmo, which is listed in the National Historic Register, is located at 426 Main Street; phone (970) 325-4951 or (866) 243-1502; www.stelmohotel.com.

There's No Place like Dome

Pagosa Springs

While many cities have annual homes tours, Pagosa Springs hosts an annual domes tour. That's dome as in geodesic dome. The ones in Pagosa are used as greenhouses, usually to transform a short mountain growing season into a 365-day-a-year pursuit.

Growing Spaces, the company behind the geodesic greenhouses, was started by former dentist Udgar Parsons, who developed the solar-powered domes while working for John Denver's Windstar Foundation in Snowmass. Although the work at Windstar involved big bucks, Parsons was able to devise an affordable geodesic greenhouse in 1998. Since then, he has built more than 500 dome greenhouses in thirty states, including several used at schools and on Indian reservations.

Proud dome owners in Pagosa Springs, where Parsons's Growing Spaces business is located, open their domes for the public to get a peek inside. At last count, there were more than seventy geodesic greenhouse domes in Archuleta County, including a community

★ ★

garden dome in downtown Pagosa, twin domes on local Enchanted Valley Farms, and the dome owned by Rio Blanco Farms that produces state-certified organic greens, sprouts, wheatgrass, and other organic products for local restaurants.

Growing Spaces is located at 1830 Majestic Drive. For more information, check out www.growingspaces.com, or call (800) 753-9333.

Year-round vegetables at 7,000-feet elevation.
Growing Spaces

Touched by a Snow Angel

Salida

The Angel of Shavano is nothing if not flexible. Although this 700-foot snow angel appears on 14,229-foot Shavano Peak for only a month or two each spring, she comes in handy for many a legend, no matter what your religious persuasion.

If Christianity is your cup of tea, you can choose between the legend that says the snow angel first appeared the year Ute chief Shavano, the mountain's namesake, decided to convert to Christianity or the one that claims she first appeared after a major labor dispute was settled after weeks of prayer. For a while, believers even made pilgrimages to see the snow-filled gulley with her arms outstretched.

Those in the Roman mythology camp claim she was Jupiter's doing. According to that legend, the Italian sky god turned one of his goddesses into ice until the valley below needed her.

The one I like best is the Indian princess legend. It seems the Indian god of plenty promised to end the drought that was driving locals out of their homeland if one of their princesses sacrificed herself. I guess the generous princess got the last laugh, because the tribe she protected is long gone, but she's still here every June spilling her tears—the melting snow—on the land below.

Of course, I'd be remiss if I didn't also mention those skeptics who claim the snow couloir known as the Angel of Shavano looks more like Woody Woodpecker or the Grinch.

No matter what your persuasion, the multitalented angel has a campground, a 7.9-mile hike, an annual Salida car show, and a classical CD named after her.

To see the Angel of Shavano that appears in June, take US 50 out of Salida and look to the right. If you want information about the Angel of Shavano Campground, call (719) 549-3591.

★ ★

Not So Silent Night
San Luis

The Reverend Pat Valdez of the San Luis diocese figured out a way to keep his parishioners out of the mall—at least during the nine days before Christmas: Get them to reenact Joseph and Mary's difficult journey from Nazareth to Bethlehem.

Actually, his scheme wasn't new. Las Posadas (it means "the inns"), as the tradition is called, has been celebrated in Mexico since the sixteenth century, when St. Ignatius Loyola substituted the nine-day Christian novena for a nine-day celebration of the birth of the Aztec sun god.

At dusk on the nine evenings before Christmas, bundled-up parishioners meet for a half-mile processional to one of nine adobe missions in the Culebra River Valley, all churches in Father Pat's parish. Children portraying Joseph and Mary, complete with a donkey (one year the donkey bucked off the Virgin Mary), lead the parade of candle-carrying adults who sing the ancient Spanish songs of Las Posadas. Unlike Mary and Joseph, who were refused respite, the good folks of Father Pat's parish let the beggars in and even ply them with their best posole, tamales, and stews at a potluck each night after the prayers.

Trivia

Quite possibly the world's largest water fight is held every year in Silverton. This annual event is held on the Fourth of July between the Silverton San Juan Volunteer Fire Department and the Animas Fire Department and takes place at the intersection of Greene and Fourteenth Streets.

* *

Agriculture—NOT

Silverton

Lots of towns have rhubarb festivals. There's one in Wakefield, England; Camden, Maine; and Cooperstown, New York, to name a few. But the International Rhubarb Festival in Silverton, Colorado, is by far the most unlikely, especially when you figure San Juan County, the county in which Silverton sits, is the only county in the entire United States without a single acre of agricultural land.

In fact, rhubarb and horseradish are the only two crops that will even grow in a backyard garden, since the growing season (days between killing frosts) lasts a mere fourteen days.

Of course, that doesn't deter Silverton's Friends of the Library from sponsoring an annual International Rhubarb Festival each Fourth of July. Right after the big parade, all sorts of unusual rhubarb dishes are offered, with all proceeds benefiting the Silverton Public Library.

Besides a rhubarb festival, San Juan County has several other rare distinctions. It has only one town (Silverton), it has a total population of 558 (compare that to New York, which has 67,000 people in every square mile), it has the cleanest air in the United States (documented by a government research station at Molas Pass), and it has the highest mean elevation of any county in the United States.

But talk about knowing how to turn lemons into lemonade. Tiny little Silverton manages to not only host the International Rhubarb Festival, but it also has its own ski hill (Silverton Mountain, 6 miles north of town, is one of the only "extreme" terrain ski areas serviced by a chairlift), its own theater company, its own history museum, and at least a dozen outdoor adventure companies.

Bat Masterson once served as the Silverton town marshal, a term that was brief. He ended up breaking more laws than he enforced. Another rumor that has yet to be substantiated is that an impoverished songwriter was sitting in a local bar when a miner's wife walked in looking for her husband. When the barkeeper said he hadn't seen him, she allegedly replied, "If he comes in, you tell that S.O.B. there's

★ ★

going to be a hot time in the old town tonight." The songwriter jotted her remark down and turned it into a tune.

For more information, write the Silverton Area Chamber of Commerce at P.O. Box 565, Silverton, CO 81433; phone (800) 752-4494; or visit www.silvertoncolorado.com.

Grateful Sled
Silverton

Yes, they own cars in Silverton. But with average yearly snowfalls of 150 inches, most residents prefer to travel the town's snow-slicked roads by kicksled, a snazzy dogsled-looking contraption with 6-foot runners, especially since locals get a wholesale discount from the guy who designs and handcrafts them at his shop on Greene Street, the main drag.

"It takes longer to scrape your windows than it takes to hop on your sled and go," says Elyse Salazar, the town administrator, who takes her sled to work, to the grocery store, and to the Avalanche coffee shop, where she parks it next to other Scandinavian-inspired kicksleds that glide like skateboards on streets the town purposely forgets to plow.

In 2002, after Brice Hoskin, a former journalist with a degree in Mandarin Chinese, overheard his wife comment that she wanted a wooden sled, he decided to design and build her one. Twenty thousand handmade sleds later, his Mountain Boy Sledworks employs seven, has twenty sales reps, and receives bulk orders from such places as LL Bean, Sak's Fifth Avenue, Plough and Hearth, and a jewelry store in Little Rock, Arkansas. Diane Sawyer bought one for weatherman Mike Barz of *Good Morning America.*

"Just don't take them down Catholic Hill," Hoskin says, referring to a street with St. Patrick's church at the top.

For those, you need Mountain Boy's Ultimate Flyer or one of his growing catalog of slope-bombing retro sleds, each made from exotic woods, then signed and numbered.

"Sleds are the eddy against the tide of all that is slick, digital, and electronic," says Hoskin, whose business card reads simply "Sledmaker."

He's probably going to be forced into reprinting or at least hand lettering a new title on the card. In May 2008 he and his wife began distilling rum. Their small-batch Montanya Distillers, operating from an old brothel on Blair Street, offers two types of rum that, so far, has mostly gone down the gullets of the town's 531 residents.

Mountain Boy Sledworks is located at 1070 Greene Street; call (800) 989-5077 or visit www.mountainboysleds.com.

A Religious Shrine That Works

One cold Sunday afternoon in January 1958 at a Catholic men's club meeting, it was suggested that they ought to build a shrine, anything to help the flagging mining economy. With donations from the owner of the Old Fisher Brewery and guidance from the parish priest, the Reverend Joseph Halloran, a 12-ton statue of the Virgin was placed in a native stone alcove on the slope of Anvil Mountain. Not six months after the shrine's dedication, the American Tunnel was built, providing access to the lower reaches of Sunnyside Mine and launching one of mining's most profitable periods in Silverton.

Later, St. Patrick's Parish purchased 1,000 Scotch pine seedlings to place behind the shrine. Locals claimed they'd never grow at that location. But just look at the mini-forest behind the shrine and ask yourself, miracle or not?

★ ★

Where's Kevin Costner When We Need Him?
Tincup

Tincup in Gunnison County may look like a ghost town (Colorado, after all, has more ghost towns than any other state), but it has managed to survive since 1861, when a miner named Ben Gray dipped his tin drinking cup into a stream for a cold one. Before he could put the cup to his lips, the thirsty miner noticed there was "gold in that thar' cup."

The crowds, the gamblers, and the millionaire wannabes followed. In just a few years, the lawless town went through eight (count 'em) marshals. Since they were hired by the gamblers with strict instructions to "see nothing, hear nothing, do nothing," they didn't last too long. The first quit, the second was fired, the third was gunned down, the fourth was shot by a gambler, the fifth quit and became a preacher, the sixth went insane, and the seventh was shot. The eighth, I'm happy to report, managed to keep his job until the town, like many mining towns, practically died in the early 1900s.

In the 1950s a radio personality from Golden, Colorado, named Pete Smythe appointed himself as mayor for eternity of "East Tincup," a fictional town much like Garrison Keillor's Lake Wobegon. Using folksy western humor and made-up folks like Moat Watkins and Elmy Elrod, the DJ who had previously written skits for Edgar Bergen and Bing Crosby turned East Tincup into a household name.

People began flocking. Today, Tincup survives thanks to summer anglers, hunters, and a log cabin cafe named Frenchy's that supposedly serves the best burgers west of the Mississippi.

Tincup is located at the south foot of the Cumberland Pass approximately 6 miles southeast of Taylor Reservoir. Cumberland Pass, built in 1882 to connect Tincup with the Denver–South Park Railroad in Pitkin, is the highest paved standard-car road in the country.

index

index

★ ★

index

index

index

247

index

index

index

index

index

★ ★

index

about the author

****

Pam Grout is a mother, a playwright, an activist, and a collector of quotes and quirky information. She has written fifteen books, including three for *National Geographic*. She writes an award-winning travel column called "Now, Where Was I?," is a stringer for *People* magazine, and has been published by the *Washington Post, Family Circle, Ladies' Home Journal, Scientific American Explorations,* and many others. For more information about Pam's books, her second career as a speaker, and her outside-the-box view of reality, check out her sometimes-updated Web site at www.pamgrout.com.